ON THIS DAY IN HISTORY

SIMON MAYO &
SIMON JENKINS

Illustrated by Martin Chatterton

An Armada Original

On This Day in History was first published in the UK in 1989 in
Armada

Armada is an imprint of the Children's Division, part of the
Collins Publishing Group, 8 Grafton Street, London W1X 3LA

Printed and bound in Great Britain by William Collins Sons &
Co. Ltd, Glasgow

The Dullest Page Ever

Well, not really, but 'Preface' isn't the most exciting way to start a book now is it? Thank you for getting this far...

I've always loved history. It didn't matter whether it was my Dad's stories, Mr Corrin's lessons at Worthing High School or Professor Berghahn's lectures at Warwick University, facts, dates and arguments were always fascinating.

Now this isn't exactly a history textbook (I'm not expecting the Open University to stock it) but it's a start! If you look hard, you'll find one of those annoying 'deliberate mistakes' somewhere in the book...

Grateful thanks to Pete Powell, Russ Lindsay and the source of all useless facts - Simon Jenkins.

On This Day in History is consistently one of the most popular features on Radio One's Breakfast Show. I hope you like the book just as much.

Name

January gets its name from one of the ancient Roman gods - the god Janus. Janus was the god of doors and the god of beginnings. He was the god you prayed to if you were starting a new business or trying out a new chariot for the first time.

Statues of Janus showed a man's head with two faces - one looking backwards, the other, forwards.

Red Letter Days

- 1 January is New Year's Day
- 6 January is Twelfth Night, the official end of Christmas
- 20 January is St Agnes' Eve, when women are said to dream of their future husband
- 25 January is Burns Night in Scotland

In our calendar, there are quite a few 'new years'. For accountants, it starts on 1 April. For texmen, it's 6 April. The new school year starts at the beginning of September. In medieval times, while most people thought of 1 January as the start of the year, the new year *officially* started on 25 March. It was only in 1752 that 1 January officially became New Year's Day in England and Ireland. It was not until 1972, 220 years later, that it was made a bank holiday.

Today is a 'dismal day'. This is one of 24 days throughout the year that were thought to be unlucky in medieval times.

1 January 1788 saw the first publication of an exciting new newspaper - *The Times*.

New Year's Day 1961 was the day when farthings ceased to be legal tender. The farthing was a quarter of an old penny, nearly one tenth of our 1p.

For centuries in Britain, there was a superstition about the first person to enter your house in the first few minutes of the new year. If the first person was a woman, had fair hair or flat feet, carried a knife, or had eyebrows which met in the middle, then it could mean bad luck for your house all year. Flat-footed knife-carrying blondes usually stayed indoors...

In medieval times, this day was known as 'the Feast of Fools' in the church. High officials of the church swopped places with the lower ones, a mock pope was elected, religious rituals were parodied and everyone generally let rip. An irreverent time was had by all.

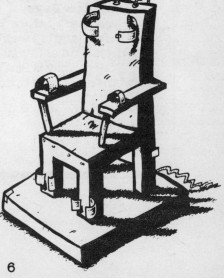

On this day in 1889, the State of New York adopted the electric chair for capital punishment.

January 1st was the birthday of **J Edgar Hoover**, founder and head of the FBI, 1895. It was also **EM Forster's** birthday, 1879. He was a famous English novelist, author of *A Room With a View*, and other novels.

hic!

JAN
2

On this day in 1900, Queen Victoria wrote her famous saying...

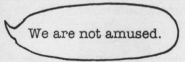

We are not amused.

On 2 January 1971, disaster struck at Ibrox Park football stadium in Glasgow. A few seconds before the end of the match, as fans were already leaving, an equalizing goal was scored. The fans surged back into the ground, crushing 66 people to death.

On this day in 1987, Golliwogs were banned from

Enid Blyton's Noddy books by their publisher, Macdonald. Golly had become an embarrassment because he was treated in the books in a racist way.

Bye Bye Golly.
Bye Bye Noddy.

Today in 1901, Britain's first municipal crematorium was opened by the Lord Mayor of Hull.

JAN 3

On this day in 1521, Martin Luther, the first Protestant, was excommunicated by Pope Leo X. Luther had defied the authority of the Pope, who now booted him out of the Catholic Church. This was the start of the split between Protestants and Catholics.

Today is the birthday of **JRR Tolkien**, creator of hobbits, the wizard Gandalf, Bilbo Baggins and vicious man-eating spiders. Tolkien, author of *The Lord of the Rings* and *The Hobbit*, was born in South Africa in 1892.

Today is also the birthday of

Victoria Principal, actress in *Dallas*. She was born in 1945.

On this day in 1795, **Josiah Wedgewood**, originator of the famous blue-and-white Wedgewood pottery, died in Staffordshire.

3 January 1946 saw the hanging in London of **William Joyce**, known as 'Lord Haw Haw'. During World War 2, Joyce made radio propaganda broadcasts for the Nazis from Germany, aimed at undermining British morale. Joyce was caught by two British officers in Denmark who recognized his voice from the broadcasts.

JAN 4

Travelling at 276mph across Coniston Water in the Lake District, Donald Campbell's jet-propelled boat *Bluebird* lifted into the air, somersaulted and smashed into the water. The disaster happened on this day in 1967 while Campbell was

attempting the world speed record on water. His body was never found. His final words were spoken over the radio...

> She's going, she's going...I'm almost on my back...

Less dramatically, **TS Eliot**, poet and author, died on 4 January 1965. His classic of children's poetry, *Old Possum's Book of Practical Cats,* inspired the musical *Cats.* 'T Eliot' spelt backwards is 'toilet'.

Today is the birthday of... **Isaac Pitman** deviser of Pitman's shorthand system, born 1813.

JAN 5

Today is the feast day of one of the most eccentric saints - St Simon Stylites, who died in Syria around AD459. Simon became so famous for his saintliness that he tried to escape from the crowds that flocked to see him by living on top of a 60-foot stone pillar. He stayed there for 39 years, but failed to shake off his fans, who gathered at the foot of the pillar.

Today's birthdays... **Jan Leeming**, the BBC newscaster. She was born on this day in 1942. **King Camp Gillette**, the American inventor of the safety razor. He was born in 1855.

Peter Sutcliffe, the Yorkshire Ripper, was charged on this day in 1981 with the murder of his final victim. A long-distance lorry driver, Sutcliffe had murdered 13 women over a four-year period.

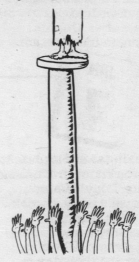

JAN 6

Today is Christmas Day in Ethiopia. The Ethiopian Orthodox Church has always celebrated the birthday of Jesus Christ on this date.

Rowan Atkinson, the comic actor, was born today, 1955.

On this day in 1928, the Thames burst its banks, flooding London and drowning four people. The Thames Barrier was still over 50 years away in the future...

6 January is one of Henry VIII's six wedding anniversaries. On this occasion, in 1540, he got married to Anne of Cleves - who he couldn't stand the sight of. When he first saw her, he remarked...

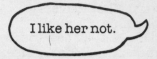

I like her not.

Also died on this day: **Theodore Roosevelt**, 26th President of the United States, 1919 **Victor Fleming**, Director of *The Wizard of Oz,* 1949.

Tonight is Twelfth Night, the final celebration of the Christmas period. Traditionally a cake was baked, with a bean and a pea buried inside it. The man who found the bean was King for the night, and the woman was Queen.

JAN 7

7 January is a sexist day. It used to be known in England as 'Distaff Day', when women went back to work after Christmas. Men returned between one and six days later, on Plough Monday, the first Monday after Twelfth Night.

One woman who didn't return to work on this day in 1536 was **Catherine of Aragon,** who died instead. Catherine was Henry VIII's first wife, but he didn't really miss her. He was already married to the second of his six wives, Anne Boleyn.

On this day in 1610, Galileo announced his discovery of four moons circling the planet Jupiter (Io, Europa, Ganymede, Callisto). He found them by using his latest invention - the telescope. The announcement caused a storm of controversy.

Today in 1961 saw the first broadcast of *The Avengers,* starring Patrick McNee as John Steed. Steed's three female companions were in turn Catherine Gale, Emma Peel and Tara King.

Today is the birthday of **Elvis Presley**, the king of rock'n'roll. He was born in Mississippi in 1935.

This is also a birthday for rock musician **David Bowie**. He was born in 1947.

On this day in the year 794, Danish Vikings attacked the island of Lindisfarne. They destroyed the famous church there before they were repelled and later shipwrecked.

We remember two popes on this day...
Pope Celestine III died today in 1198. Celestine was a powerful pope - he once kicked the German Henry VI's crown off his head while Henry was kneeling before him, just to emphasize who really held power in Europe. **Pope Pius X** today banned Catholic women from wearing low-cut dresses in the presence of church dignitaries, 1904.

And two deaths...
Robert Baden-Powell, founder of the Boy Scout Movement, 1941.
Galileo Galilei, astronomer and physicist, 1642. His last words were a protest that the Earth moves around the Sun, and not the other way round, as the church claimed:

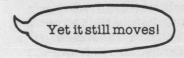

Yet it still moves!

JAN 9

On this day in 1969, *Concorde,* the world's first supersonic airliner, was given its first trial flight at Bristol. Developed jointly by Britain and France, there had been an argument over whether or not the aircraft's name should have a final French 'e'.

On 9 January 1957, Anthony Eden resigned as Britain's Prime Minister.

On this day in 1806, Lord Nelson, hero of the Battle of Trafalgar, was buried at St Paul's Cathedral.

The first film to receive the new 'X' rating opened on 9 January 1951 in London. Titled *Life Begins Tomorrow,* it received its rating for a scene dealing with artificial insemination.

Today is the birthday of **Richard Nixon,** 37th US President, 1913. One of his most famous lines...

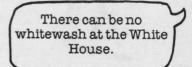

There can be no whitewash at the White House.

JAN 10

The 'Penny Post' was introduced in Britain by Rowland Hill on this day in 1840. Before the Penny Post, the person who *received* the letter had to pay for it.

On this day in 1985 Sir Clive Sinclair's ill-fated C5 took to the road. This battery-operated tricycle is now about as popular as platform soles.

10 January is a birthday for the rock star **Rod Stewart.** Rod was born in 1945.

These people died on the 10th of January...
William Laud, Archbishop of Canterbury, supporter of

King Charles I. Laud was beheaded at Tower Hill in 1645.

Samuel Colt, American gunsmith and inventor, 1862.

Coco Chanel, fashion designer who gave her name to the perfume Chanel No.5, 1971.

Buffalo Bill, (William Cody), frontiersman and showman, 1917. He was called Buffalo Bill because he once potted nearly 5000 buffalo over an 18-month period. His last words, spoken on this day, were...

> Well, let's forget about it and play High Five. I wish Johnny would come.

JAN 11

On this day in 1864, Charing Cross station in London was opened.

Today's birthday boys...
Arthur Scargill, the National Union of Mineworkers leader. Arthur was born in 1936.

Harry Gordon Selfridge, 1864. In 1909, Harry founded Britain's first department store, Selfridge's, in London's Oxford Street. On opening it, he said:

> The great principles on which we will build this business are as everlasting as the pyramids.

The novelist **Thomas Hardy** died today, 1928, in Dorset. One of his most famous novels is *Tess of the D'Urbervilles*.

Can't *wait* for the next invasion...

JAN 12

On this day in 1970, a Boeing 747 Jumbo Jet touched down at Heathrow Airport for the first time. The newly-developed Jumbo was on its maiden transatlantic flight from New York.

Today's birthdays are... **Michael Aspel**, television presenter and chat-show host. He was born in 1933. **Joe Frazier**, world heavyweight boxing champion in the 1970s. Joe was born today in 1947. **Hermann Goering**, born today in 1893. Goering was the commander of the Luftwaffe (German air force) during World War 2.

The British-Zulu war began on this day in 1879.

The crime fiction writer **Agatha Christie** died today in 1976 - in unsuspicious circumstances.

JAN 13

On this day in 1957, Elvis Presley recorded *All Shook Up* in a Hollywood studio.

13 January 1982: During a snowstorm, an Air Florida jet took off from Washington National Airport. The plane immediately plunged into the frozen Potomac river in the heart of Washington, near the White House. Despite rescue attempts, the icy river claimed over 80 lives.

Three famous people died on 13 January... **George Fox**, founder of the Quakers, 1691. **Wyatt Earp**, famous marshall of Dodge City, died in his sleep, 1929. **Charles the Fat**, (son of Charles the Bald), ruler of the Holy Roman Empire, 888.

JAN 14

Lewis Carroll, creator of *Alice in Wonderland,* died on this day in 1898. His real name was the Revd. Charles Dodgson.

A new invention, the 'telephone', was today demonstrated to Queen Victoria at Osborne House on the Isle of Wight, 1878.

Edmund Halley, of 'Halley's Comet' fame, died on this day, 1742. Halley observed his comet in 1682 and predicted its return in 1759. Unfortunately he wasn't around to see that he had been proved right.

Walt Disney's epic, *Snow White and the Seven Dwarfs,* went on general release on 14 January 1938.

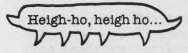

Heigh-ho, heigh ho...

Humphrey Bogart, film star and cult personality, died on this day, 1957.

JAN 15

Today is the birthday of **Martin Luther King**, now a public holiday in the US. King was born in 1929.

On this day in 1867, the ice on the lake in Regent's Park seemed strong enough for skating and walking. When the ice gave way, 40 people never made it out of the freezing waters alive...

Another disaster took place today in 1877. Due to torrential rain, the railway tunnel connecting Dover and Folkestone collapsed. Fortunately, no one was seriously hurt.

President Sadat of Egypt opened the Aswan High Dam on this day in 1971. The dam keeps the level of the River Nile constant throughout the year.

Edward Teller, 'the father of the H-Bomb', was born in Budapest on this day in 1908.

James Joyce, the Irish novelist, died on this day, 1941.

JAN 16

In the United States, 16 January 1920 marked the start of the Prohibition era. The manufacture and sale of alcohol was banned for the next 13 years.

Born today...
André Michelin. Born in Paris, 1853, Michelin built the first factories for mass-produced rubber tyres. The singer **Sade** was born on this day in 1960.

On this day in 1780, British admiral George Rodney defeated the Spanish at Cape St Vincent. They had been attacking British forces stationed on Gibraltar.

This day in 1932 saw the recording of *It Don't Mean a Thing* by the giant of jazz, Duke Ellington.

JAN 17

On this day in 1977, **Gary Gilmore**, a convicted murderer, was shot by firing squad in Nevada, USA. He was the first convict to be executed in the US for over ten years. He had campaigned *in favour* of his execution, and his final

words were...

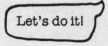

Let's do it!

Today's birthday boys...
Lloyd George, British Prime Minister and subject of the song *Lloyd George knew my father*... Born in 1863. **Muhammad Ali**, world

heavyweight boxing
champion, 1942.

The first ship ever to cross
the Antarctic Circle did so on
this day in 1773. The ship
was Captain Cook's
Resolution.

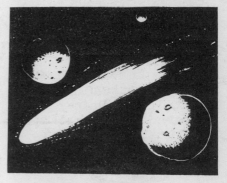

JAN 18

On this day, Halley's Comet
was first spotted on its 1910
visit to the Sun. The comet,
which has been described as
'a dirty snowball' with a tail
millions of miles long, visits
the Sun every 76 years. Its
last appearance was in 1986.

Whose birthday is it?
AA Milne, author of *Winnie-
the-Pooh*, 1882.
David Bellamy, naturalist
and larger-than-life
television personality. Born
in 1933.

On 18 January 1936,
Rudyard Kipling died.
Kipling was a famous poet,
and author of *The Jungle
Book*. When Walt Disney
made his film version of the
book, he handed it to one of
his animators and told him…

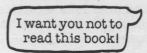

I want you not to
read this book!

JAN 19

19 January is one of those days in history on which not a lot happened. For Mrs Poe and Mrs Cézanne, however, it was a productive day:

Paul Cézanne, famous French artist, was born this day in 1839

Edgar Allan Poe, master of spine-chilling stories, was born this day in 1809. One of Poe's most famous short stories is the horrific *The Pit and the Pendulum*.

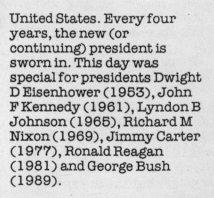

heh heh heh!

JAN 20

Today is St Agnes' Eve. In medieval times this was popularly believed to be the day on which a woman could find out who her future husband would be. Whoever she dreamed about (even if it was the village frog) would be The One. Some men tried to fix it so that their name came up.

Today is also Presidential Inauguration Day in the United States. Every four years, the new (or continuing) president is sworn in. This day was special for presidents Dwight D Eisenhower (1953), John F Kennedy (1961), Lyndon B Johnson (1965), Richard M Nixon (1969), Jimmy Carter (1977), Ronald Reagan (1981) and George Bush (1989).

On this day in 1965, DJ **Alan Freed** died in California. He was the creator of the phrase 'rock'n'roll'.

18

On this day in 1878, Cleopatra's Needle arrived in London after a long and troubled sea-voyage from Egypt. The 3500-year-old obelisk started its voyage from Alexandria in a specially-built vessel, the *Cleopatra*, the previous September and was temporarily lost in a gale in October.

King Edward VIII came to the British throne today in 1936, on the death of his father, George V. He was to rule for only 11 months.

JAN 21

On this day in 1793, at the start of the French Revolution, **King Louis XVI** was guillotined in Paris for treason. Just before taking his last breath, he said...

> I shall drink the cup to the last dregs...

On this day in 1987, Terry Waite, the Archbishop of Canterbury's special envoy, was kidnapped by a terrorist group. He was in Beirut to negotiate for the release of other kidnap victims.

Today's births...
Billy Ocean, born in 1952.
Christian Dior, French fashion designer, 1904.
Benny Hill, naughty comedian and singer of smash hit *Ernie*...

> He drove the fastest milk-cart in the West...

Benny was born in 1924.

Today's deaths...
Vladimir Ilyich Lenin, leader of the 1917 Russian Revolution, 1924.
Cecil B de Mille, Hollywood film producer, California, 1959
George Orwell, author of *1984* and other novels. He died in 1950. Among his last words were...

> At fifty, everyone has the face that he deserves.

JAN 22

On this day in 1901, **Queen Victoria** died at the age of 81. She had ruled since 1837, longer than any other British monarch (63 years, 216 days).

The first ever Labour government was formed under the leadership of Prime Minister Ramsay MacDonald on this day in 1924.

22 January 1972 marks the entry of Britain into the EEC. As Prime Minister Edward Heath entered the Egmont Palace to sign the agreement, he was splattered with ink by a woman who was demonstrating about something else...

Today in 1983, tennis star Bjorn Borg took early retirement. He had reached the grand old age of 26!

On this day in 1879, the heroic battle of Rorke's Drift took place. A handful of British soldiers under the command of lieutenants Chard and Bromhead successfully resisted a large Zulu army.

JAN 23

On this day in 1960, the deepest point on Earth was reached. Jacques Piccard and Donald Walsh, in their bathyscaphe *Trieste,* touched down on the ocean floor in the Marianas Trench, 6.78 miles deep. They made it back alive.

23 January is the birthday of **Humphrey Bogart**. The film star was born in 1899. Bogart's most famous line...

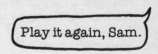

Play it again, Sam.

William Pitt the Younger, who became Britain's youngest-ever Prime Minister at the age of 24, died in London on this day in 1806. His last words were…

> I think I could eat one of Ballamy's veal pies.

JAN 24

On this day in 1916, the US Supreme Court ruled that Income Tax was unconstitutional.

Today is the birthday of the Roman Emperor **Hadrian**. He was born in Spain in the year AD76, and is famous for building Hadrian's Wall.

24 January 1966: an Air India Boeing 707 crashed into Mont Blanc, killing all 117 passengers on board.

Sir Winston Churchill died on this day in 1965. On his 75th birthday, 15 years earlier, Churchill had said…

> I am ready to meet my Maker. Whether my Maker is prepared for the ordeal of meeting me is another matter.

JAN
25

Today the church remembers the conversion of St Paul. Paul started out as an infamous persecutor of Christians, but he was converted during a journey to Damascus when he was knocked off his horse and blinded by a great light. In medieval England, the weather on this day was said to forecast the weather throughout the year.

Tonight is 'Burns Night' in Scotland, commemorating the birth of the national poet, Robert Burns, in 1759. It's a great night for wearing your kilt, eating haggis, singing *Auld Lang Syne* and reciting some of the great man's poetry.

25 January is Henry VIII's wedding anniversary. But as Henry was married no less than six times, which anniversary was this? Today in 1533, Henry secretly married the gorgeous Anne Boleyn in Whitehall. Unfortunately, neither the marriage nor Anne lasted very long.

Today was a 'Dismal Day' in the Middle Ages. It was considered an unlucky day.

Today's birthday persons are both English novelists... **Virginia Woolf**, author of *To the Lighthouse*, 1882. **Somerset Maugham**, author of *The Moon and Sixpence*, 1874.

On this day in 1905, the largest diamond ever discovered came to light in the Premier Diamond Mine, Pretoria, South Africa. It was named 'the Cullinan' and presented to King Edward VII.

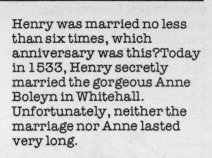

JAN
26

On this day in 1841, Hong Kong was proclaimed British sovereign territory and became a colony of the British Empire.

In medieval times, London's River Thames repeatedly froze over in winter, allowing 'frost fairs' to be held on the thick ice. The most recent frost fair ended when the ice thawed out on this day in 1814.

General Gordon, the famous British soldier, was killed on 26 January 1885 at Khartoum in the Sudan. He had been trying to help the Egyptians fight the Mahdi.

Today is the birthday of the actor **Paul Newman**. He was born in 1925.

JAN 27

In 1926, on this day, John Logie Baird gave the first-ever public demonstration of his new invention - television. With the aid of two unpleasant-looking ventriloquist's dummies, the first flickering pictures were transmitted.

Today is the birthday of...
Wolfgang Amadeus Mozart, composer extraordinaire. Mozart was born in 1756. By the age of six he was composing his first pieces of music.
Lewis Carroll, the author of *Alice in Wonderland* and *Through the Looking Glass*. Carroll (whose real name was Charles Dodgson) was born in 1832.

On this day in 1923, the first Nazi rally was held in Munich. It was led by an unknown corporal from the First World War, Herr Adolf Hitler.

Who died on this day?
Bartolommeo Cristofori, who developed the first piano, 1731.
Philippe Buache, inventor of contour lines on maps, 1773.

Three US astronauts also died today in 1967. **Gus Grissom, Ed White** and **Roger Chaffee**, were rehearsing an *Apollo* mission when a flash fire broke out in the capsule on their launch pad. Grissom was the second US astronaut in space, in 1961.

The River Thames caught fire on this day in 1906. It ignited due to oil pollution.

JAN 28

On this day in 1986 the Space Shuttle *Challenger* was launched from Cape Canaveral, USA. Only 73 seconds into its flight, it exploded at a height of 47,000 feet, killing all seven of its crew members.

Sir Francis Drake, defeater of the Spanish Armada, died on board his ship on this day in 1596.

On 28 January 1788, the first penal colony was founded in Australia at Botany Bay. Many thousands of convicted criminals were sent to Australia from Britain before transportation was abolished in 1864.

Today saw the death of three great kings...
Charlemagne (which means 'Charles the Great'), Holy Roman Emperor, 814.
Peter the Great, dynamic ruler of Russia, 1725.
Henry VIII, 1547. Henry's last words were...

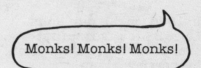

Monks! Monks! Monks!

Henry was survived by his sixth wife, Catherine Parr, who went on to marry again.

JAN 29

At 8pm on this day, 1616, Cape Horn was rounded for the first time by the Dutch ship *Unity*, commanded by Captain Schouten. They had a typically rough ride.

On this day in 1856, the Victoria Cross was instituted by Queen Victoria. The medal was to be given for conspicuous bravery in wartime. Each one was originally cast in metal taken from cannons captured during the Crimean War.

A new military invention was tested out at Hatfield today in 1916. Its code-name was 'the tank'.

Desert Island Discs was first broadcast on 29 January 1942 by Roy Plomley. He died on 30 May 1985 after hosting 1,791 programmes.

King George III died on this day, 1820. George remains the longest reigning British king, ruling for 59 years and 96 days. Queen Victoria beat him to first place as the longest-reigning British monarch.

JAN 30

On this day in 1649, **King Charles I** was beheaded in Whitehall, London. His death warrant was signed by Oliver Cromwell and 58 others. He wore two shirts to his execution as it was a cold day, and he didn't want the onlookers to think that he was shivering from fear.

This day also saw the assassination of **Mahatma Gandhi**, who secured independence from British rule for India, in 1948. His killer, a Hindu fanatic, stepped out of a crowd and shot him three times.

Orville Wright, the first man to fly in a heavier-than-air machine, died today, 1945.

Adolf Hitler became Chancellor of Germany and formed a Nazi cabinet on 30 January 1933. He was only to relinquish the power he took on this day when he committed suicide in 1945.

Today was 'Bloody Sunday' in Ulster, 1972. British Paratroopers opened fire during a civil rights demonstration, killing 13 men and boys.

JAN 31

On this day in 1606, **Guy Fawkes** and his fellow-conspirators were executed by being hanged, drawn and quartered.

Bonnie Prince Charlie, also known as 'the Young Pretender', died in Rome on this day, 1788. Charles was leader of the Scottish Jacobite Rebellion, aimed at deposing King George II. This failed and he became an alcoholic in his old age.

Today's birthdays...
Franz Schubert, 1797. He was the composer of the 'Unfinished' Symphony.
Phil Collins, formerly the drummer with *Genesis*, and now rock musician in his own right. Born in 1951.

The ship, the *Great Eastern*, built by Isambard Kingdom Brunel, was finally launched today in 1858. But it was hardly a triumph. The launch had began almost three months earlier, but the ship was so massive that it got stuck on the slipway and refused to budge.

On this day in 1867, the statue of Lord Nelson, plus the four lions at the base of Nelson's column, were unveiled at Trafalgar Square.

JANUARY QUIZ

1. What do the Scots do on Burns Night (25 January)?
a) toss the caber
b) eat haggis
c) celebrate hogmanay

2. The infant Jesus had some visitors on 6 January. Who were they?
a) the three wise men
b) the twelve disciples
c) the shepherds

3. What service started on 7 January 1857?
a) London postal service
b) London Omnibus service
c) The first Kissogram

4. King Louis XVI was guillotined on 21 Jan 1793. What were his last words?
a) 'I do this for my country'
b) 'I will drink the cup to the last dregs'
c) he said nothing

5. What is 6 Jan also known as?
a) Plough Monday
b) Black Death Day
c) Old Christmas Day

FEBRUARY

Name
February is named after the little-known Roman god Februus. *Februa* is a latin word meaning 'to purify'. On 15 February in Roman times there was a festival of purification.

Originally in the Roman calendar there were only ten months (March to December). But in 713BC, King Numa Pompilius of Rome added January and February to top up the calendar to its present 12 months.

Red Letter Days
• 14 February is St Valentine's Day
• 29 February is Leap Year Day - it is only included in February every fourth year.

FEB 1

February 1st, the 32nd day of the year, marks the feast day of St Ignatius of Antioch. St Ignatius, who died around AD115, was desperate to be martyred for his faith in the Roman arena. He even planned to entice the wild beasts to devour him, just in case they didn't feel too hungry. In the end, he didn't have to bother...

burp!

On this day in 1911, Mr Edward Mylius was sentenced to one year in prison. His crime? He had accused King George V of being married to several women.

Today's birthdays...
Clark Gable, Hollywood film star from *Gone With the Wind* and other film greats, Born 1901.
Stanley Matthews, the footballer, born 1914.

This day also marks the death of the author **Mary Shelley**. Back in 1818 she wrote a little book called *Frankenstein*. She died in 1851. No bolt was discovered through her neck.

On this day in 1966, the silent film comedian **Buster Keaton** died.

FEB 2

On this day in 1917, during World War 1, bread rationing started in Britain.

On 2 February 1971, Major-General Idi Amin, the psychopathic ruler of Uganda, pronounced that he was absolute ruler 'for ever and ever' of that country. He later also declared himself ruler of Scotland and generously offered to marry Princess Anne to heal the rift between Uganda and Britain.

Today is the birthday of **Nell Gwynne**. Born in 1650, Nell was an actress, and Charles II's best-loved mistress. She started her career as a barmaid, but as Charles' mistress received £4000 a year plus a house in Pall Mall.

Today's birthdays...
Farrah Fawcett, the American actress, born in 1946.
Les Dawson, comedian and perfector of the mother-in-law joke. Born in 1933.

Today is St Blaise's Day. If your cough medicine fails, you can try praying to St Blaise, as he's reportedly brilliant at healing illnesses of the throat. Animals used to come to him for healing, so he is also seen as the protector and healer of animals. Especially animals with a bad throat.

Today is the anniversary of the first controlled landing of a man-made object on the Moon. The Soviet spacecraft *Luna IX* achieved a soft landing on this day 1966, and sent back to Earth the first TV pictures from the Moon's surface.

This is a day for musical birthdays. **Felix Mendelssohn**, composer (born 1809), shares this day with **Val Doonican**, singer and model for exotic sweaters (born 120 years later).

On this day in 1488, Bartholomew Diaz became the first European to discover the Cape of Good Hope, South Africa. His first go at naming it was 'Cape Tormentosa', which means 'Stormy Cape', but his Portuguese boss King John II renamed it.

On 3 February 1959, **Buddy Holly**, rock'n'roll pioneer, was killed when his plane crashed in the US. The lyrics from one of his most famous songs say it all...

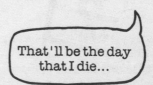

That'll be the day that I die...

29

FEB 4

Today is St Veronica's Day. According to Catholic legend, she mopped the sweat from Jesus's face as he carried his cross to the place of execution in Jerusalem. When she looked at the handkerchief she had used she was astonished to find his face imprinted on it. The Vatican claims to have the handkerchief...

The first Sunday colour supplement was published on this day in 1962. The newspaper was the *Sunday Times,* and it was widely expected that the magazine section would flop.

Today is a 'Dismal Day'. In medieval England, this day (plus 23 others throughout the year) were believed to be unlucky.

Today is the birthday of **Charles Lindbergh**, born in 1902. Lindbergh was the first person to fly solo across the Atlantic, from New York to Paris. He was 25 years old.

I wonder what time the in-flight movie starts?

FEB 5

This day saw the first-ever edition of the *Reader's Digest,* 1922.

5 February is also the birthday of **Sir Robert Peel**, born 1788. Robert Peel, Britain's Home Secretary, was the founder of the Metropolitan police force. The new policemen were quickly nicknamed 'bobbies' and 'peelers' after Sir Bob.

Walt Disney's animated film, *Peter Pan,* went on general release on this day in 1953.

Today is also the birthday of **John Dunlop**, born in 1840. He developed the first commercial pneumatic tyre, after helping his kid to win a tricycle race by putting inflated tubes on his wheels (surely cheating?).

On this day in 1811, the Prince of Wales became Prince Regent, ruling in the place of his father, King George III. King George had taken to talking with trees in Windsor Great Park and to furniture in the castle, and had been declared insane.

Today's birthdays...
Ronald Reagan, starring actor in *Bedtime for Bonzo* and 40th US President. Born 1911.
Eva Braun, mistress to Adolf Hitler and his wife for the last hours of his life. Born 1912.

On this day in 1685, James II became king. Exactly 267 years later (in 1952) Elizabeth II also came to the throne. She didn't know that she had become queen for two days, as she was staying in Treetops Hotel (a hotel literally built in a group of trees) in Kenya.

On 6 February 1918, British women were allowed the vote for the first time. But you had to be over thirty. Over 21-year-olds had to wait until 1928 before they could vote.

Today marks the death of **Adolphe Sax**, 1894, inventor of the saxophone.

On this day 1969, Marvin Gaye's *I Heard it Through the Grapevine* was released in Britain.

Today's birthday boys... **Thomas More**, Lord Chancellor in the time of Henry VIII and author of the book *Utopia*. After his death Thomas was made a saint, and has the dubious honour of being the only English saint ever to have owned a pet monkey. Born 1478. **Charles Dickens**, the great Victorian novelist, author of *Oliver Twist* and other classics. Born in Portsmouth, 1812.

On this day in 1974, after 85 days in space, the American crew of the orbiting station *Skylab* returned to Earth for a change of clothes...

Today is St Jacqueline's Day. She kept a pet lamb that was incredibly pious. Apparently the lamb would wake her for her prayers in the mornings if she had overslept...

This is your early-morning call...

Mary Queen of Scots was beheaded on this day in 1587 at the order of her cousin Elizabeth I. Just after the axe fell, Mary's pet terrier ran out from under her dress, where it had been hiding.

Today's birthdays include...
Chester Carlson, inventor of xerox copying. Born 1906.

Jules Verne, author of *Twenty Thousand Leagues Under the Sea, Around the World in Eighty Days,* and others. Born 1828.
James Dean, American heart-throb film star. Born 1931.

FEB
9

Bill Haley, trail-blazing rock'n'roller, singer of the legendary *Rock Around the Clock*, died on this day in 1981.

Today in 1969, the new 747 Jumbo Jet was given its first trial flight.

On 9 February 1942, during World War 2, soap-rationing began. Meanwhile, back in World War 1, on this day in 1916 conscription started because young men were volunteering at a slower rate than soldiers were dying.

On this day in 1555 during the reign of 'Bloody' Mary, the Bishop of Gloucester, **John Hooper**, was burned at

the stake for heresy. His last words were...

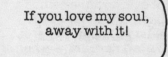

If you love my soul, away with it!

FEB 10

On this day in 1912, **Robert Scott** and his two fellow-explorers were found dead in their tent in Antarctica. They were returning from their journey to the South Pole, and were just eleven miles from safety.

This day in 1944 was a dark day for wage packets. Pay-as-you-earn income tax was introduced in Britain.

Today is the birthday of **Samuel Plimsoll**, 1824 (inventor of the 'plimsoll line' on ships), **Boris Pasternak** 1890 (Russian author of *Dr Zhivago*), and **Harold Macmillan** 1894 (British Prime Minister).

This date marks two royal murders. In 1400, **King** **Richard II** mysteriously 'disappeared' while imprisoned at Pontefract Castle, Yorkshire. And in 1567, Mary Queen of Scots' husband, **Lord Darnley**, was murdered as he lay ill in bed. His house was blown up and he was then strangled. Who did it? Was Mary herself involved? The mystery has never been solved...

10 February 1956. Elvis Presley walked into a recording studio and recorded his first record, *Heartbreak Hotel*...

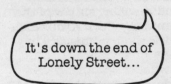

It's down the end of Lonely Street...

FEB 11

11 February is a good day for Catholics. On this day in 1929 the Vatican was declared an independent state after a treaty was signed between Pope Pius XI and the Italian leader Mussolini.

On this day in 1975, Margaret Thatcher became leader of the Conservative Party. She was the first woman ever to lead a British political party. She went on to become Britain's first woman Prime Minister in the General Election of 1979.

Today is the birthday of... American inventor **Thomas Edison**, 1847. Edison invented the record player, the electric light bulb and an early kind of movie camera. **Burt Reynolds**, American film star. He was born on this day in 1936.

FEB 12

On this day in 1797, the last invasion of the British mainland took place. General Tate, an Irish-American, landed at Carreg Gwasted in Pembrokeshire with over 1400 French troops. They later surrendered to Lord Cawdor's soldiers, plus a group of locals brandishing pitchforks.

Can't wait for the next invasion...

Today's birthday boys were both born on the same day in the same year. They were: **Abraham Lincoln**, probably the best-known US President. **Charles Darwin**, of evolution fame. Both were born in 1809.

On this day in 1818 Chile declared its independence.

12 February 1924 saw the first performance of George Gershwin's *Rhapsody in Blue*. The jazz piece, which Gershwin wrote mostly during a train journey, stunned its New York audience.

On this day in 1554, **Lady Jane Grey** was executed on Tower Hill. Jane had been crowned Queen but was imprisoned after only 11 days because of popular support for her cousin Mary.

Today in 1961, Dr Albert Crary reached the South Pole. He was the first man to stand on both North and South Poles (but not at the same time). He had been on the opposite side of the Earth nine years previously.

Today is the anniversary of the infamous Glencoe Massacre of 1692. The Campbell clan had enjoyed two weeks of caber-throwing and whisky while staying with the MacDonalds. Then suddenly, early one morning, they turned on their hosts and killed them in their beds. This later caused a spot of tension between the Campbells and MacDonalds.

On this day in 1867, Johann Strauss's *Blue Danube* waltz was first performed in Vienna.

This day was also special for Mr Arthur Hyne, a dentist. Today in 1908, he was sentenced to seven years in prison for bigamy. He was married five times over.

Catherine Howard, the teenage wife of Henry VIII (his fifth), was executed on this day in 1542. They had been married for just eighteen months. Only a year earlier Henry had showered Catherine with diamonds, rubies and pearls.

On this day in 1689, King William III and Queen Mary II came to the British throne. They ruled the country jointly.

It's been popular to send the one you love a card on St Valentine's Day since the 17th century. St Valentine himself has no obvious connection with the romantic side of life, but this date was fixed in medieval times because people then believed that birds began to mate on the 14th!

On this day in 1931 Groucho Marx and his family were strip-searched in customs when entering New York. It all happened because Groucho, impatient at the delays, asked his wife in a loud voice:

Have you got the opium?

On 14 February 1975 the author and creator of 'Jeeves', **PG Wodehouse**, died.

Captain James Cook, who explored the Australian coast and many Pacific islands, was murdered on this day, 1779, by the natives of Owhyhee, Hawaii.

Today is also the anniversary of the infamous St Valentine's Day massacre, which took place in Chicago in 1929. Seven gangsters were lined up against a beerhouse wall and shot by members of Al Capone's gang.

FEB 15

On this day in 1971, Britain changed over to decimal coinage. The centuries-old currency system in which there were 12d in a shilling and 20s in a pound officially ended. The d became p and the half crown was dead. And everyone was very confused...

On this day in 1942, the war was going badly for the Allies. Singapore, crucial to the British, fell to the Japanese army...

But on the same day in 1945, the war was going a lot better. British troops finally reached Germany's River Rhine, forcing the Germans to retreat inside their own territory.

Today's birthdays...
Galileo Galilei. Born in 1564, Galileo was the first to use the telescope. He was kept under house arrest during his final years for teaching the revolutionary idea that the Earth goes around the Sun, rather than vice versa. **Harold Arlen,** born in New York, 1905. Arlen was the composer of the song *That Old Black Magic*.

On this day in 1944, during World War 2, the Allies began the bombing of Monte Cassino, where Italian forces were holding the ancient monastery. The monastery was completely flattened.

FEB 16

On this day in 1960, the US nuclear submarine *Triton* set off on the first underwater voyage around the world without surfacing.

Today is the birthday of **John McEnroe**, tennis star. John made his first noises on 16 February 1959.

On this day in 1801, William Pitt resigned as Britain's Prime Minister. Meanwhile, on this day in 1959, Fidel Castro became Cuba's Prime Minister.

This date marks the death (on dry land in 1834) of **Lionel Lukin**, inventor of the lifeboat.

On 16 February 1933, England won the ashes against Australia after the controversial 'bodyline' tour. England's fast bowlers had bowled at the batsmen's legs and body, making the game dangerous. It simply wasn't cricket.

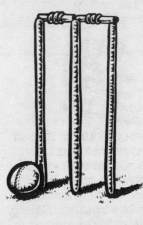

FEB 17

On this day in 1905, the Russian **Grand Duke Sergei** was assassinated when a nail bomb was lobbed into his lap as he was being driven into the Kremlin.

On this day in 1956, the first episode of *The Adventures of Robin Hood* appeared on TV. The series starred Richard Greene as our hero. The famous signature tune entered the Top 20 and the series ran to an amazing 143 episodes.

Today's birthday persons... **Dame Edna Everidge** (Barry Humphries), born 1934 **Gene Pitney**, the singer of *24 Hours from Tulsa* and other

hits, born 1941)
René Laënnec, French army doctor whose claim to fame is that he invented the stethoscope. He first christened the new instrument the 'breast explorer'! Born in 1781.

On 17 February 1923, Lord Carnarvon opened the inner tomb of the Egyptian King Tutankhamen at Luxor. The tomb had been sealed since 1337BC.

Today in 1967 the Beatles' *Penny Lane / Strawberry Fields For Ever* single was released.

FEB 18

On this day in 1930, the planet Pluto was first discovered. Pluto is the furthest planet from the Sun and takes 248 years to complete just one orbit.

On this day in 1516, Henry VIII was bitterly disappointed. His wife gave birth to a daughter, and Henry was desperate for sons. His daughter grew up to become Queen Mary, who gave her name to the drink 'bloody Mary'.

Born on this day...
Count Alessandro Volta. Born in 1745, he was the inventor of the battery. Electrical 'volts' are named after him.

Yoko Ono also celebrates her birthday on this day. She was born in Tokyo in 1933.

On this day in 1678, John Bunyan's *Pilgrim's Progress* was first published. It immediately topped the best-seller lists.

Died on this day...
Michelangelo, the Italian sculptor, painter and architect. Michelangelo is particularly remembered for his painting *The Last Judgment,* in the Sistine Chapel, Rome. Died 1564.
Richard Wagner, the German composer. Died in 1883.
'Gentleman Jim' (his real name was James Corbett). He was a famous boxer, and died in 1933.
Robert Oppenheimer, father of the Atom Bomb. Died 1967.

FEB 19

Today is St Conrad of Piacenza's Day. St Conrad is invoked for the cure of hernias, but he also knew about an effective way to cure temptation. Whenever he saw a beautiful woman, he would roll among thorn bushes as a form of gentle distraction.

Under massive pressure from America, the USSR on this day in 1963 agreed to remove its forces from Cuba. The world breathed again. For a while, everyone thought that this was The End.

Prince Andrew, now the Duke of York, was born on this day in 1960.

On this day in 1878, Thomas Edison patented his invention, the 'phonograph' (record player). For those who like details, the patent number was 200521.

FEB 20

On this day in 1861 the steeple of Chichester Cathedral was blown down in a great storm.

20 February 1962 marks the launch of astronaut John Glenn in *Friendship 7* - the first American spacecraft to orbit the Earth. As Glenn passed over Perth, Australia at night, most of the population of the city turned their lights on so that he could see them.

On this day in 1811, Austria declared itself bankrupt.

The 'Cato Street Conspiracy' was discovered on this day in 1820. The conspiracy was to

40

assassinate the Prime Minister and his cabinet, but Arthur Thistlewood and his fellow-plotters were discovered, and eventually hanged.

New £10 notes were issued in Britain on 20 February 1975. One side shows Florence Nightingale carrying a lamp while she attends to wounded soldiers during the Crimean War.

FEB 21

On this day in 1903, it rained blood on the South of England. The 'blood' was later discovered to be ordinary rain, coloured by dust blown over from the Sahara Desert.

On this day in 1436, Scotland's **James I** was murdered. And in 1965, **Malcolm X**, the radical black Muslim leader in America, was also killed. Meanwhile, **Jethro Tull**, the English agricultural pioneer, died quietly at home in 1741.

21 February 1863 was the day when the Post Office started a new mail bag service. It ran beneath London's streets, powered by pneumatic conveyors.

Today's birthdays...
WH Auden, the English poet, was born in 1907.
Cardinal Newman, the 19th-century convert to Catholicism, was born in 1801.

FEB 22

Today is Thinking Day. At least, that's what Boy Scouts call this day. 22 February is the birthday of their founder, **Robert Baden-Powell**, born in 1857.

The tallest man known was born on this day in 1918. **Robert Wadlow** was born in Illinois, USA and grew to a height of 8ft 11ins by his death at 22.

Other birthdays include...

Bruce Forsyth, television game-show host. Brucie was born in 1928.
George Washington, first President of the United States. Born in 1732.
Frederic Chopin, the Polish composer and pianist. Born in 1810.
Luis Buñuel, Spanish film director. Born in 1900.

On this day in 1804, Richard Trevithick drove the first steam engine to move on rails in front of an excited crowd in Penydarren, Wales. The engine pulled a train of wagons filled with men.

FEB 23

This day in 1968 marked another great milestone in musical history. Tom Jones unleashed his song *Delilah* on an unsuspecting world.

Four gloomy days in history occurred on this date. On this day, the following four people died...
Stan Laurel, the thin half of the comedy duo Laurel and Hardy, died in 1965.
LS Lowry, the north-of-England painter renowned for painting matchstick men and women, died in 1976.
John Keats, the romantic young poet, died of tuberculosis in Rome. Keats, who was 25, died in 1821. Keats asked that his gravestone should say...

> Here lies one whose name was writ on water.

Andy Warhol, the pop-art painter died in New York, 1987. Some of his followers refused to believe it and thought he would turn up during his own funeral. He didn't.

To balance things up, there were also some births...
Samuel Pepys (his surname is pronounced Peeps) the racy diary writer, was born this day in 1633.
George Frederick Handel, German composer of *The Messiah*, was born in 1743.

Alleluia!

FEB 24

Today is St Matthias' Day. Matthias was one of the early disciples of Jesus. After Judas had betrayed Jesus and had committed suicide, Matthias was selected to replace him in the group of twelve disciples. He was the only disciple to be chosen by casting lots (ancient dice-throwing).

One of the world's best-known train services, the *Flying Scotsman,* went into service on this day in 1923.

24 February 1902: London's first telephone service was opened.

On this day in 1582, Pope Gregory announced to the world in general that the ancient Roman calendar, used by most of Europe, was out of step with the seasons by 10 days. He called all countries to 'lose' 10 days and start a new calendar system, the 'Gregorian' calendar. The Catholic countries obeyed, but other countries refused. Britain and the Protestant American states stayed with the old calendar until 1752, while Russia held out until 1918.

FEB 25

Today's birthday boys...
George Harrison, guitarist with the Beatles, born in Liverpool, 1943.
Zeppo Marx, the Marx Brother who was given all the straight lines in their movies, born in New York, 1901.
Pierre Renoir, French impressionist painter, born in Limoges, 1841.

Sir Christopher Wren, the architect, died on this day in 1723. Sadly he popped off before his masterpiece, St Paul's Cathedral, was completed. His tomb in St Paul's reads: 'If you seek his monument, look around.'

'Bluebeard', the French murderer, was guillotined on this day in 1922. **Henri**

Landru was found guilty of murdering ten women, luring them to their fate with adverts in the lonely hearts columns of newspapers. Henri gave himself away by leaving a diary detailing the crimes in his flat.

On this day, 1964, Cassius Clay became world heavyweight boxing champion by beating Sonny Liston with a mixture of brilliant boxing, dodging, and screamed insults. Clay later changed his name to Muhammad Ali. He was not noted for his humility...

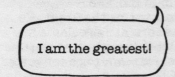

I am the greatest!

FEB 26

Today is a 'Dismal Day'. In medieval England, this day (plus 23 others throughout the year) were believed to be unlucky.

The first-ever issue of £1 and £2 banknotes took place in England on this day, 1797.

On this day in 1936, Adolf Hitler opened the first factory for a new German car - the 'People's Car' (or in German, 'Volkswagen').

Unusually, the engine was at the back, and was air-cooled.

On 26 February 1815, Napoleon escaped from the island of Elba, off the coast of Italy. He had been banished there by the French for losing a war with Austria.

Today's birthdays...
Sandie Shaw, 1947, pop

singer from the sixties who used to sing in her bare feet. **Victor Hugo**, 1802, author of many books, including *The Hunchback of Notre Dame* ...

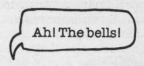

Ah! The bells!

FEB 27

Today is the birthday of the Roman Emperor **Constantine the Great**. He was born in Yugoslavia in AD280. Constantine was the first emperor to be converted to Christianity, and he made it the empire's official religion.

In 1939, on this day, Borley Rectory was burned to the ground. It was known as England's most haunted house.

Six years earlier to the day, in 1933, Berlin's Parliament building, the Reichstag, was also burned down. Hitler had just come to power, and he blamed his political enemies, the Communists, for arson.

However, there was a secret tunnel connecting the Reichstag to the house of Nazi leader Hermann Goering...

This day in 1900 saw the founding of the British Labour Party.

The continent of Antarctica was first discovered on this day in 1831 by Captain John Briscoe.

Aaaargh! It's snapped!

FEB 28

On this day in 1912, the first successful parachute drop from an aeroplane was made by Albert Berry, in Missouri, USA.

That's another failed suicide bid...

John Wesley founded Methodism today in 1784.

28 February 1975: the Moorgate tube disaster killed 42 passengers. It was London Underground's worst ever train crash. The train shot through platform nine of Moorgate station without stopping and rammed into a dead-end tunnel.

The Labour Party won the General Election this day, 1974. But their victory was slightly spoiled by their slim majority - just 4 seats.

The Swedish Prime Minister, **Olaf Palme**, was assassinated in Stockholm on this day in 1986. He was gunned down by a lone sniper as he and his wife walked home from a night out at the cinema.

Today's birthdays include...
Charles Blondin, Niagara Falls tightrope walker, 1824.
Barry McGuigan, world featherweight boxing champion, 1961.

FEB 29

Today is Leap Year Day. For a year to contain a 29 February, it has to be divisible by four. Everyone knows that. But a lesser-known fact is that century years have to be divisible by 400 to be a Leap Year. So 1900 had no 29 February, but 2000 will. Leap Years occur because each year contains just under 365.25 days. The extra day in every fourth year keeps us in step with the seasons.

Officially a Leap Year contains 365 days, 28 and 29 February being seen as two days in one. Government departments and insurance companies treat them as such and people celebrate their birthday on 28 February in non-Leap Years.

In sexist days of yore, women were allowed a one day in four years chance to propose marriage to men on this day.

On this day in 1968, the first pulsar (pulsating radio source) was discovered, by Cambridge boffins.

29 February 1792 is the birthday of the composer **Rossini**. Rossini composed *The William Tell Overture*). As he was born on Leap Year Day, 1992 will be his 50th birthday.

On this day in 1868, Benjamin Disraeli became British Prime Minister. His comment...

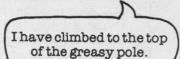

I have climbed to the top of the greasy pole.

1. What did Hitler usually give his mistress, Eva Braun, on her birthday (6 February)?
a) expensive jewellery
b) cheap jewellery
c) hamsters

2. What happened on 8 Feb when Queen Mary was beheaded?
a) they discovered she was a man
b) the executioner passed out
c) her red-haired wig fell off

3. The gangster Al Capone ordered the St Valentine's Day Massacre, 14 Feb 1929. What was 'Al' short for?
a) Alan
b) Albino
c) Alphonse

4. What was nationalized on 14 February 1946?
a) the Bank of England
b) British Rail
c) British Steel

5. What did John McEnroe (born 16 Feb) call a tennis referee in 1985?
a) 'bird brain'
b) 'dumbhead'
c) 'the pits of the world'

Answers on page 272

47

MARCH

Name

March was the first month in the ancient Roman calendar. The name comes from Mars, the god of war. The Romans were a warlike race, which is why they named their first month after the god of war. 'Mars' has found his way into our language - 'martial arts' and 'martial law' both come from this Latin word.

Julius Caesar's reforms to the calendar in 46BC turned March into the third month of the year.

Red Letter Days

- 1 March was New Year's Day for the ancient Romans - now it is St David's Day for the Welsh
- 17 March is St Patrick's Day, celebrated by the Irish
- 21 March is the Spring Equinox
- 25 March is old New Year's Day

1 March is St David's Day, celebrated in Wales by people wearing leeks and eating daffodils (or should that be the other way round?). St David is the patron saint of Wales, traditionally thought to be King Arthur's uncle.

Today is a 'Dismal Day'. In medieval England dismal days were considered unlucky.

On this day in 1845, Texas became part of the United States. In the 10 years before this date it had been an independent country.

1 March 1954 marked the second H-Bomb test by the United States, at Bikini Atoll in the Pacific. The blast was equivalent to 12 million tons of TNT, 600 times more powerful than the Hiroshima bomb. Japanese fishermen, who saw the explosion from 70 miles away, thought the sun was rising.

Today was New Year's Day in ancient Rome. March was the first month of the year until January and February were added in 713BC.

Today's birthdays include...
Glen Miller, famous American bandleader during World War 2, born 1904.
David Niven, English film actor, born 1910.

On this day in 1965, *The Sound of Music* went on general release in America. It was an instant hit.

Today is **Mikhail Gorbachev's** birthday. Leader of the Soviet Union, he was born in 1931.

On this day in 1836, 59 citizens of Mexico founded the independent republic of Texas. After a war with Mexico, Texas became a US state in 1845.

Today marks the day when three men finally kicked the bucket. They were...

DH Lawrence, the English novelist. He is most famous for his novel *Lady Chatterley's Lover*, which was banned in Britain until 1960. Lawrence died of tuberculosis in Nice on the same day that Mikhail Gorbachev was being born, 1931.

Howard Carter, who discovered the tomb of King Tutankhamen in Egypt. Despite the curse on the tomb door, Carter died 17 years after entering it, in 1939.

John Wesley, founder of worldwide Methodism. Wesley shocked the church of his day by preaching in the streets to the massive crowds that came to hear him. It is estimated that he travelled over 250,000 miles on horseback on his preaching tours. He died in 1791, aged 87. Wesley once said...

I look upon all the world as my parish.

On this day in 1788, the **'Young Pretender'** died in Rome. Charles Edward Stuart was the grandson of King James II, and claimed to be heir to the British throne. Unfortunately, King George II was comfortably seated on the throne at the time. Charles led an unsuccessful Scottish invasion of England in 1745 (known as the Jacobite Rebellion), which reached as far south as Derby. Charles Edward eventually died in Rome as an alcoholic.

3 March 1861 marked the abolition of serfdom (a form of slavery) in Russia. Serfdom had ended in England by the 17th century.

Today's birthday persons... **Ursula Andress**, film actress, born 1936. **Alexander Graham Bell**, Scottish-born inventor of the telephone, born 1847.

This date is a good one for Hollywood. For a start, Walt Disney's classic, *Cinderella,* was released, this day in 1950. It is also **Marlon Brando's** birthday, the legendary film star, born in Nebraska, 1924. And this is also the day on which Charlie Chaplin was knighted by the Queen, 1975.

On this day in 1861, Abraham Lincoln became 16th President of the United States. He was the first US president to have a beard. He was also the first to be assassinated.

Saladin, the legendary Muslim commander during the Crusades, died in Damascus today in 1193. He survived many battles and at least two assassination attempts, but died of natural causes.

Today's birthdays...
Antonio Vivaldi. Born in Venice, 1678, Vivaldi became a prolific composer, producing 40 operas, 23 symphonies and over 400 concertos. No one much cared about Vivaldi's music until he was rediscovered in the 1930s.
Prince Henry the Navigator. Born 1394. Henry was the Portuguese prince who started off the European 'discoveries' of the African and Indian coasts. Before Henry, hardly any Europeans knew they were there.

The Forth Rail Bridge (crossing the Firth of Forth in Scotland) was opened on this day, 1890.

MARCH 5

On this day in 1936, the Spitfire was given its maiden flight in Southampton. The plane was decisive in winning the Battle of Britain in the summer of 1940.

On 5 March 1953, **Josef Stalin**, leader of the Soviet Union, died in Moscow. His real surname was Djugashvili, but he chose Stalin as it is the Russian word for steel. He was a fearsome ruler. It is estimated that he had more people put to death in Russian concentration camps than Adolf Hitler.

This day is also memorable for Ronnie and Reggie Kray, much-feared gang leaders in London's East End. On 5 March 1969 both twins were given 11 sentences for murder and jailed for a minimum of 30 years each.

Gerard Mercator, the famous cartographer, was born this day, 1512. He is remembered for his map of the world, known as the 'Mercator Projection'.

On this day in 1946, Winston Churchill coined the phrase 'the iron curtain' in a speech. Talking about the Soviet Union, he said...

An iron curtain has descended across the Continent.

MARCH 6

Two icy disasters happened on this day...

In 1906, an avalanche at Roger's Pass in the United States buried a snow train. By the time the train had been dug out, 62 lives had been lost.

In 1987, on this day, the cross-channel ferry, the *Herald of Free Enterprise,* capsized a few minutes after it had left the safety of Zeebrugge. The bow doors had been left open, allowing the car deck to be covered with a sheet of water a few inches deep. This was heavy enough to turn the ferry over. Over 200 people died in the icy waters.

On this day in 1836, **Davy Crockett**, US frontier folk-hero, died at the Battle of the Alamo in Texas. He and the entire garrison of 150 soldiers were killed by 4,000 Mexican troops, who were trying to regain Texas as part of Mexican territory.

Today's birthdays include... **Elizabeth Barrett Browning**, famous Victorian poet. She was born in Durham in 1806. **Michelangelo**, the great Italian artist, sculptor and architect. He is particularly famous for his paintings on the ceiling of the Sistine Chapel. Born 1475.

John Philip Sousa died on this day, 1932. Sousa was the American composer of the military-sounding music that started *Monty Python's Flying Circus.* The music is called *The Liberty Bell.*

MARCH 7

On this day in 1976, a family of three in Timberville, USA, got the shock of their lives. As they watched TV during the evening, a block of ice the size of a football suddenly hurtled through their roof and a plasterboard ceiling to smash on the floor in front of them. Inexplicably, a second block landed in the road only 50 metres away 20 seconds later. The incidents were never explained.

On 7 March 1882, a Bill was read in Parliament to prevent atheists becoming MPs. It failed.

On this day in 1936, the world moved several steps closer to World War 2. Hitler's troops reoccupied the west bank of the River Rhine, something they had been forbidden to do since World War 1.

Today's birthday persons...
Rik Mayall, actor in *The Young Ones,* was born this day in 1958.
Ivan Lendl, the tennis player, was born today in 1960.

MARCH 8

On this day in 1917, **Count Ferdinand von Zeppelin** died. He was the builder of the first successful airship. Zeppelins were used to bomb Britain during World War 1.

Today is **Kenneth Grahame's** birthday. The author of *The Wind in the Willows,* starring the Rat, the Mole, and the famous Mr Toad, Grahame was born in Edinburgh in 1859.

Anyone seen my cigarette lighter?

MARCH 9

Today would have been the Russian cosmonaut **Uri Gagarin's** birthday. Born in 1934, Uri became the first man in space in 1961. Unfortunately he died in a plane crash in 1968.

On this day in 1796, Napoleon Bonaparte married Joséphine de Beauharnais. This was probably *not* the day on which he said his famous remark:

Not tonight, Joséphine...

MARCH 10

On this day in the year 515BC, the Jewish Temple in Jerusalem was completed. Originally built by King Solomon over 400 years earlier, it had been destroyed during an invasion by the ferocious Babylonians.

London's Bakerloo Tube line was opened today in 1906.

On 10 March 1974, a Japanese soldier was discovered on Lubarg Island, in the Philippines, wearing World War 2 battle gear. He thought that the war was still in progress, nearly 30 years after it had finished.

This day marks the beginning of Hollywood history. 10 March 1910 saw the release of the first Hollywood movie, called *In Old California*.

This day also saw the release of Sandie Shaw's *Puppet on a String,* in 1967. The song went on to win the Eurovision Song Contest.

On this day, 1813, Frederick William III of Prussia instituted the Order of the Iron Cross. These medals were presented to honour 'patriotic bravery in the war against France'.

MARCH 11

On this day in 1938, Hitler invaded Austria and made it a province of Germany. He went on to invade Czechoslovakia and Poland, provoking World War 2.

Also on this day, in 1985, Mikhail Gorbachev became supreme leader of the Soviet Union, the most powerful man in the East.

11 March 1955 marks the death of **Sir Alexander Fleming**. He was the Scottish bacteriologist who discovered penicillin in 1928.

London's first daily newspaper, the *Daily Courant*, was first published on this day, 1702.

On 11 March 1845, self-raising flour was first patented by Mr Henry Jones of Bristol.

Born on this day...
Rupert Murdoch, inventor of Page 3 Girls, owner of the *Sun*, The *Times*, Sky Television and assorted publishers (including the publisher of this book). Rupert was born in Australia in 1931.
Harold Wilson, pipe-smoking Prime Minister of Britain in the 1960s and mid-1970s. Born in Huddersfield, 1916. Wilson once said...

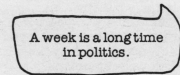

A week is a long time in politics.

MARCH 12

On this day in 1945, **Anne Frank**, the Dutch-Jewish girl who hid from the Nazis in Holland, and wrote her famous Diary, died in the Bergen-Belsen concentration camp. She and her family had hidden in sealed-off rooms for two years at the top of a building in Amsterdam. Only 34 days later the concentration camp was liberated by the allies.

Today is **Thomas Augustine Arne's** birthday. Born in London in 1710, he was the composer of *Rule Britannia*.

On this day in 1781, the astronomer Sir William Herschel discovered the planet Uranus. Sir William had the bright idea of calling the new heavenly body *Georgium Sidus,* in honour of King George III. But eventually the planet was given its much more sensible name.

Still on the discovery of planets, the discovery of Pluto, the planet furthest from the Sun, was announced this day in 1930.

13 March 1867: The United States bought Alaska from Russia for the knock-down price of $7.2m, or $12.28 per square mile. When oil was discovered in Alaska, there were some green faces in the Kremlin.

This day in 1968 witnessed the release of Cliff Richard's Eurovision Song Contest winner, *Congratulations.*

On this day in 1758, Halley's Comet reached its closest point to the Sun - just as predicted by Edmund Halley back in 1682. Halley died 16 years too early to see himself proved right.

MARCH 14

This day in 1868 saw the founding of the very first US professional baseball club. The team were the Cincinatti Red Stockings.

Todays birthdays...
Michael Caine, British film actor, was born in 1933. 'Not many people know that...'
Jasper Carrott, stand-up comedian, born today, 1945.
Albert Einstein was born this day in 1879, in Ulm, West Germany. Einstein started life as a patents clerk, but shot to fame as a physicist and wild-haired genius with his theory of relativity, published in 1915.

Karl Marx, philosopher and founder of Marxism, died in London on this day in 1883. When he was asked if he had any last words of wisdom to say, he shouted...

Get out!

On this day in 1891, the first underwater telephone cable was laid on the bed of the English Channel by a ship called the *Monarch*.

MARCH 15

15th March in the Roman calendar was known as 'the Ides of March'. On this day in 44BC, the Roman Emperor Julius Caesar was assassinated in the Roman Senate House. Julius coined the famous remark:

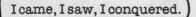

I came, I saw, I conquered.

On 15 March 1909, Mr GS Selfridge opened Britain's first department store in London - Selfridges. The shop had six acres of space.

On this day in 1493, Christopher Columbus arrived home in Spain after his first voyage to the New World. He was still convinced that he had been to India, rather than to America.

On this day in 1895, **Bridget Cleary**, aged 27, was burned to death at Baltyvadhen,

County Tipperary in Ireland. This was the last-known burning to death for witchcraft in the British Isles.

Rebecca West, the feminist author died today in 1983. She once said...

> There is of course no reason for the existence of the male sex except that one sometimes needs help in moving the piano.

Not a lot happened on this day in history. However, Britain did get a new translation of the Bible. On 16 March 1970, the newly-completed *New English Bible* first went on sale. It sold one million copies in its first day.

Today is St Patrick's Day. Patrick is the patron saint of Ireland, but he is big in America, too. In New York, an annual parade down Fifth Avenue takes place on St Patrick's Day.

On this day in 1649, during the rule of Oliver Cromwell, kingship in England was abolished. But it didn't last long. Eleven years later, in 1660, Charles II became king.

This day was popularly regarded in the Middle Ages as the day when Noah and his family (plus a few assorted animals) entered the ark.

Today is **Rudolf Nureyev's** birthday. He was born in 1938. A famous Soviet ballet dancer, Nureyev defected to the West in 1961.

On 17 March 1984, a funny thing happened at the Oxford & Cambridge Boat Race. While the two boats were lining up for the start of the race, Cambridge's boat was badly damaged when it hit a barge.

MARCH 18

On this day in 1932, the Sydney Harbour Bridge was opened. At the time, it was the largest single-span bridge in the world.

18 March is the anniversary of the 30mph speed limit in Britain. The limit was imposed for built-up areas on this day in 1935.

Lt-Col Aleksey Leonov went for a walk on 18 March 1965. Nothing strange about that. But the walk was done 300 miles above the Earth, and was the first-ever spacewalk. Aleksey performed somersaults during his 10-minute stroll outside his craft, *Voskhod 2*. He beat the Americans to this feat by 10 weeks.

On this day in 1834, six Dorset farm workers, known as 'the Tolpuddle Martyrs' were sentenced to transportation to Australia for swearing an oath to join a trade union. Due to public outrage, they were pardoned two years later.

Today's birthday boys...
Rudolf Diesel, born in Paris, 1858. Diesel was the inventor of diesel engines.
Neville Chamberlain, born in Brighton, 1869. Chamberlain was the Prime Minister who attempted to negotiate with Hitler, but was overtaken by the start of World War 2.

Ivan the Terrible, crowned the first Tsar of Russia, died on this day, 1584.

MARCH 19

On this day in 721 BC, the first recorded eclipse in history was observed by the Babylonians. It was an eclipse of the Moon, and was reported by the ancient astronomer Ptolemy.

Edgar Rice Burroughs, the creator of Tarzan, died on this day in 1950. Tarzan's most celebrated saying:

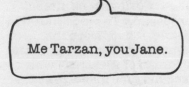

Me Tarzan, you Jane.

On this day in 1834, the Tolpuddle Martyrs were sentenced to seven years' transportation to Australia. The six men were Dorset farm workers, found guilty of belonging to a trade union - which at that time was illegal. They were pardoned two years later after a national outcry.

Today's birthdays...
David Livingstone, the African missionary and explorer. Livingstone was the first European ever to see the Victoria Falls. He was born in Strathclyde, Scotland, in 1813.
Nigel Clough, the footballer, was born on this day in 1966.

MARCH 20

The foundation stone for Dartmoor Prison was laid on this day, 1806.

On this day in 1893, the Pope sent a phonograph (an early type of record) to the President of the United States. The album didn't contain the Pope's Greatest Sermons, but a simple, friendly message.

A bleak day for Germany. On this day in 1933, the Nazis opened their first concentration camp at Dachau.

Sir Isaac Newton died in London on this day, 1727. He is famous for discovering the law of gravity, supposedly by watching an apple fall. Among his last words were:

> I seem to have been only a boy playing on the seashore and diverting myself in now and then finding a smoother pebble or prettier shell than the ordinary, whilst the great ocean of truth lay all undiscovered before me.

MARCH 21

Today is the spring equinox, when the Sun crosses over the equator, and day and night are roughly the same length.

Today is the birthday of the composer **Johann Sebastian Bach**. Bach was born in 1685, and is one of the greatest composers.

This day, 1963, saw the closure of Alcatraz, the most notorious prison in the United States. The prison was built on a small island in San Francisco Bay, and the vicious currents around the island made escape almost impossible. The most famous convicts there were the gangster Al Capone, and 'the Birdman of Alcatraz' who used his time inside to study birds doing time inside their own cages.

Thomas Cranmer, Archbishop of Canterbury in the time of Henry VIII, died on this day, 1556. Cranmer cleverly arranged Henry's divorce of his first wife, but he was put to death by her daughter, Queen Mary. Cranmer was burned to death for heresy. At first he had signed a confession that his beliefs were wrong, to avoid death. But they decided to execute him anyway. As the fire started, Cranmer held out the hand that had signed the paper, saying...

> This hand having sinned in signing the writing must be the first to suffer punishment. This hand hath offended.

MARCH 22

The first-ever demonstration of cinematograph (movie) film took place in Paris on this day in 1895. The Lumière brothers (Auguste and Louis) had developed the camera and projector, which ran at 16 frames per second.

Today is **Chico Marx's** birthday. He was born in New York in 1887. He plays the piano in Marx Brothers' movies. His real name was Leonard, but he was called Chico because of all the women ('chicks') he chased after. Chico was also a demon card-player and was notoriously late for filming sessions. One of his famous (and corny) sequences...

Chico What is it has a trunk, but no key, weighs 2,000 pounds, and lives in the circus?
Prosecutor That's irrelevant.
Chico A relephant! Hey, that's the answer!

Today is also the birthday of **Andrew Lloyd Webber**. He was born in 1948.

MARCH 23

On this day in 1925, the State of Tennessee in America declared that it was illegal to teach the theory of Evolution in schools, as it contradicted the Bible's account of the creation.

Also on the religious front, the Pope met the Archbishop of Canterbury in their first meeting for 400 years, on this day in 1966. Pope Paul VI and Archbishop Ramsey sat and talked in the Vatican's Sistine Chapel.

On 23 March 1882, polygamy was abolished in the United States. Before that you could have as many wives as you liked.

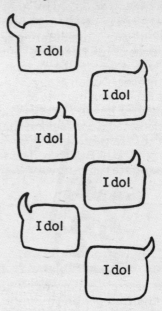

MARCH 24

A bad day for Paris. On this day in 1918, towards the end of World War 1, 'Big Bertha', a 420mm German gun, began firing shells on Paris from 65 miles away. The gun was named after Bertha Krupp, the wife of its inventor.

Today's birthday personages...
Elton Box, composer of the song *I've Got a Lovely Bunch of Coconuts*. Born in Lancashire, 1903.
Ub Iwerks, the film animator who drew Mickey Mouse for Walt Disney. Born 1901.
Steve McQueen, star of films like *The Magnificent Seven*, *Bullitt* and *The Great Escape*, in which he did all his own

stunts. Born 1930.

At 3am, this day, 1603, **Queen Elizabeth I** died at Richmond Palace. It was the last day of the year by the old way of reckoning the calendar.

This day in 1905 saw the death in France of **Jules Verne**, author of *Around the World in 80 Days*. He was 77.

Today in 1838, London's National Gallery in Trafalgar Square was opened.

MARCH 25

Today was officially New Year's Day in England from the 12th century until the calendar changed in 1752. January the 1st then took over.

On this day in 1843, the first tunnel under the Thames (linking Rotherhithe and Wapping) was opened. Built by Isambard Kingdom Brunel, it took years to complete as the tunnel frequently collapsed. It is now a tube tunnel.

Today witnessed the first showing of *Fireball XL5* on British television in 1963. The puppet characters included Steve Zodiac (commanding the spaceship), Venus, his glamorous helper, Professor 'Matt' Matic and Robert the Robot.

Over 300 years after he died, Oliver Cromwell's head was buried at Sydney Sussex College, Cambridge, on this day in 1960. His head parted company with his body in 1660.

This day in the middle ages was the Feast of the Good Thief, when people remembered the thief who died on the cross next to Jesus Christ.

Today's birthday persons... **Elton John**, rock composer and performer. Elton (real name Reg Dwight) was born in 1947.

This day marks a twin disaster for British motorists. On 26 March 1934, the British Road Traffic Act introduced the Driving Test for all motorists. And on 26 March 1958, the first parking tickets were issued to the unlucky by the new traffic wardens.

On this day, 1827, **Ludwig van Beethoven**, the deaf composer, died. His last words were...

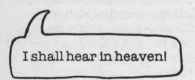

I shall hear in heaven!

Britain's first ever Sunday newspaper was published today in 1780. It was given the snappy title, *The British Gazette and Sunday Monitor.*

On 26 March 1859, Monsieur Lescarbault, a French physician, sighted a planet which seemed to be closer to the Sun than Mercury. He named it Vulcan. However, Vulcan has never officially been declared a planet, and most people now think that Lescarbault saw a stray asteroid.

David Lloyd George, former Prime Minister of Britain, died on this day in Wales, 1945.

Today is **Diana Ross's** birthday. She was born in 1944.

On 27 March 1966, the World Cup, which had been stolen a few days earlier, was discovered in a South London garden by a dog

named 'Pickles'. Four months later, England won the cup for the first and (so far) only time.

On this day in 1977, two Jumbo Jets collided on the runway at fog-bound Tenerife airport. One jumbo was taking off and had begun to lift off the ground, and the other taxied into its path.

Over 570 people never made it out alive.

MARCH 28

On this day in 1964, in the days before Radio One, Britain's first pirate radio station, *Radio Caroline*, began transmitting pop music illegally from a ship in the North Sea.

Today is a 'Dismal Day'. In medieval England dismal days were considered unlucky.

On 28 March 1542, during the reign of Henry VIII, **Margaret Davy** suffered the rare punishment in England of boiling to death. She had committed murder by poisoning.

The Oxford and Cambridge Boat Race had to be re-run on this day in 1912. There was a slight technical hitch. Both boats had sunk.

Three wars are remembered on this day...
In 1854, England and France declared war on Russia, starting the *Crimean War*.

On 28 March 1939, the *Spanish Civil War* ended when Madrid surrendered to General Franco.
And on this day, 1945, the last German V-2 Rocket landed in Britain towards the end of *World War 2*.

On this day in 1930, the city of Constantinople changed its name to Istanbul. It had also been known as Byzantium.

28 March is the birthday of **Neil Kinnock**, leader of the Opposition. He was born in Wales in 1942.

There were a number of deaths on this day...
Colonel Uri Gagarin was killed in a jet crash north of Moscow, 1968. Gagarin was the first man to travel in space, on 12 April 1961.
Dwight Eisenhower, former President of the United States, died today in 1969.
Virginia Woolf, the English novelist, committed suicide by drowning herself in a river, 1941.

MARCH 29

This day in 1652 was known as 'Black Monday', as Britain experienced a total eclipse of the Sun. Many people refused to go to work, or even to leave their homes, through fear that the darkened Sun would make them go mad. It was widely expected that terrible events were about to happen. The rich packed up and fled from London and the poor prayed that God would let them see the Sun again.

On this day in 1871, the Royal Albert Hall was opened by Queen Victoria. It was named after her husband, Prince Albert, who had died 10 years earlier.

This day, 1851, also saw London's Marble Arch moved from its position at Buckingham Palace to where it now stands at the top of Oxford Street. Wouldn't it have been easier to leave it where it was?

Today is the birthday of **Eric Idle**, film comedian and former member of the *Monty Python's Flying Circus* team. He was born in 1943.

MARCH 30

30 March 1981: President Ronald Reagan was shot in the chest during an assassination attempt. The gunman opened fire as Reagan left a Washington hotel and was stepping into his car. In hospital it was found that the bullet had passed just three inches from his heart. Before he went into the operating theatre, he asked the surgeon...

Are you a Republican or a Democrat?

Today's birthday-holders are...
Rolf Harris, Australian entertainer and cartoonist, born 1930.
Vincent Van Gogh, Dutch painter, born 1853.

MARCH 31

On this day in 1889, the Eiffel Tower in Paris was completed after taking two years, two months and two days to build. It stands 986 feet tall, and was named after Gustave Eiffel, its designer and builder.

On 31 March 1901, the first-ever Mercedes car was built for an Austrian diplomat living in Nice. The car was called Mercedes because that was the name of the diplomat's daughter.

Today saw two births...

Franz Joseph Haydn, the composer who taught both Mozart and Beethoven. Haydn also composed the German national anthem. He was born in Austria, 1732.
David Steel, leader of the Liberal Party, born in 1938.
Robert Bunsen, inventor of the bunsen burner. Born in Germany, 1811.

And two deaths...
John Constable, the English painter, died this day in 1837. Probably his most famous painting is The Hay Wain, which was considered revolutionary in its day.
Charlotte Brontë, the author of the novel *Jane Eyre*, died this day, 1855.

MARCH QUIZ

1. Which of the events of 10 March caused the onlookers to both laugh and cry?
a) the Japanese soldier
b) the Jewish Temple
c) the first Hollywood movie

2. On 13 March, Uranus was discovered. How many planets separate Earth from Uranus?
a) 4
b) 3
c) none

3. The composer JS Bach was born on 21 March. Shortly before he died, what happened to him?
a) he went blind
b) he finally became famous
c) he went deaf

4. Which of these DJs worked for Radio Caroline (started transmitting 28 March)?
a) Steve Wright
b) Peter Powell
c) Kenny Everett

5. Prince Albert was Queen Victoria's husband. What was his surname?
a) Windsor
b) Stuart
c) Saxe-Coburg

Answers on page 272

APRIL

Name
April was the second month of the year for the Romans. They called it *Aprilis*. But why was it called this?

No one really knows. Some think it was named from the Latin word *aperire*, 'to open', meaning that it was the beginning of spring. Others think it comes from the Greek goddess of love, *Aphrodite*, as the Romans dedicated this month to Venus, the Roman version of Aphrodite.

Red Letter Days
- 1 April is April Fools' Day
- 1 April is also the first day of the new financial year
- 6 April is New Year's Day for British taxmen
- 23 April is St George's Day, celebrated in England

APRIL 1

Today is April Fools' Day. Practical jokes are allowed up till noon. The origin of the day is that April 1st was often celebrated as New Year's Day in medieval times, before January 1st took over. But when New Year's Day changed to 1 January in 1752, some idiots still carried on celebrating the new year on April 1st. This amused their neighbours, who started calling them 'April fools'. At least, that's one theory of how it all started.

April 1st is still a sort of New Year's Day. It's the first day of the new financial year.

While we're on the subject of accounts, Albert Einstein, the Jewish physicist, had his Berlin bank account seized by the Nazis on this day in 1933. Fortunately, he was in America at the time.

The treadmill was abolished in British prisons on 1 April 1902.

This day in 1918 saw the formation of the RAF. The Royal Flying Corps and the Royal Naval Air Service merged to form the new force.

On April 1st 1924, Adolf Hitler was sentenced to five years in prison for high treason after a failed attempt to start a fascist revolution in Germany. In the end, he served only eight months of his sentence.

Today's birthdays...
The Russian composer **Sergei Rachmaninov**, born in 1873.
William Harvey, physician to Kings James I and Charles I, who discovered blood circulation. Born 1578.

APRIL 2

On this day in 1978, the first episode of *Dallas* was screened in America.

2 April 1982: Argentinian troops invaded the Falklands Islands. The small company of British marines was soon forced to surrender. Argentinians in Buenos Aires rejoiced at the news, while there was shock and horror in London. The invasion sparked the Falklands War.

Haile Selassie was proclaimed Emperor of Ethiopia today in 1930. Rastafarians believe that he was the Messiah, God-on-earth.

Born on this day...
Charlemagne, the Holy Roman Emperor. Born 742.
Hans Christian Andersen, the author of some of the most well-known fairy tales. *The Ugly Duckling, The Emperor's New Clothes* and *The Snow Queen* all came from his pen. Born in Denmark, 1805.
Alec Guinness, the British actor. Born in London, 1914.
Marvin Gaye, soul singer. He was born on this day in 1939.

Samuel Morse, who gave his name to the code he invented, died today in New York, 1872.

APRIL 3

On this day in 1933, two biplanes became the first aircraft ever to fly over Mt Everest.

Meanwhile, back in 1860, the first Pony Express (a mail service on four legs) set out across the United States.

On 3 April 1913, Emmeline Pankhurst, the suffragette, was sentenced to three years in prison. She had been found guilty of inciting her supporters to place explosives at the London house of cabinet member Lloyd George. Votes for women were only granted in 1918.

Born today: **Eddie Murphy**,

movie comedian. He was born this day in 1961.

Jesse James, the American bank and train robber (and folk-hero) finally bit the bullet on 3 April 1882. He was standing on a chair to straighten a picture when an accomplice walked in the room and shot him. His final words...

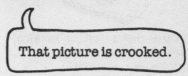

That picture is crooked.

APRIL 4

4 April 1968: Just after 6.00pm, the American civil rights leader **Martin Luther King** was shot dead on the balcony of his motel in Memphis, Tennessee. His killer, James Earl Ray, had hired a room overlooking the motel, and police found a chair by his window with the curtain slightly drawn back. Martin was 39 years old.

On this day in 1581, Francis Drake was knighted by Queen Elizabeth I.

It was announced today in 1896 that gold had been discovered in the Yukon (north-west Canada). Immediately there was a gold rush. 30,000 hopefuls swarmed to the Klondike River, to pan and mine for gold.

Today features two executions...
James Hanratty was hanged in Britain for the A6 murder, 1962.
'Galloping Dick', the highwayman, was executed in Aylesbury, 1800.

This day in 1949 saw the signing of the NATO (North Atlantic Treaty Organization) agreement by representatives of 11 countries.

Carl Benz, the early car pioneer and half of Mercedes-Benz died on this day, 1929. He built his first petrol-driven car in 1885.

On this day in 1910, kissing was banned on French railways.

This day in 1964 also saw the first trial of driverless automatic trains on the London Underground.

Winston Churchill resigned as Prime Minister on 5 April 1955. He was 80 years old and became a backbencher in the House of Commons.

Today was a good day for Hollywood. Three of its greatest actors were born...
Spencer Tracy, one of the great screen actors, star of *Guess Who's Coming to Dinner* and other films. Born in 1900.
Bette Davis, another Hollywood legend, famous in the 30s and 40s. Born in 1908.
Gregory Peck, born in 1916.

Also born today in 1724 in Venice was **Casanova** (his real name was Giovanni Jacopo) the world's greatest latin lover. In between girlfriends, he was a spy, librarian, violinist and generally had numerous adventures...

Died on this day...
Robert Raikes, the founder of Sunday Schools, 1811.
Howard Hughes, the world's most famous recluse, died while flying in his private jet, 1976.

74

6 April marks the start of the British Income Tax year. Taxmen everywhere rejoice!

On this day in 1199, **Richard the Lion Heart** died. He was attacking a castle near Chalus in France, when he received a fatal crossbow wound. It was incredibly bad luck. Only 15 poorly-equipped men were defending the castle, and the man who shot him was using a frying pan as a shield.

Robert Peary became the first person to stand on the North Pole, today in 1909. It was his sixth attempt.

A rare earthquake rocked London on 6 April 1580, during the reign of Elizabeth I. Old St Paul's Cathedral was quite badly damaged, and two people were killed.

The first Olympic Games to take place in the modern era was inaugurated by the Greek King in Athens, today in 1896.

William Wordsworth became Poet Laureate today in 1843 at the age of 73. His most well-known poem is the famous 'I wandered lonely as a cloud...' But he is also remembered for some appallingly bad lines...

'I've measured it from side to side;
Tis three feet long and two feet wide.'

Almost three years after World War 1 started, the United States joined in by declaring war on Germany. It happened on this day, 1917.

Today's births include...
Harry Houdini, the American escapologist who escaped from locked cells, handcuffs, underwater cases, straitjackets - you name it! His mum knew him as Erich Weiss. Born 1874.
John Betjeman, one of Britain's Poet Laureates. Born in London, 1906.
Maximilien de Robespierre, lawyer and leader of the French Revolution. He was born in 1758.

APRIL 7

On this day in 1739, **Dick Turpin**, the highwayman, was executed in York. He was hanged for cattle-stealing and smuggling, as well as for holding up stage-coaches.

Today is the most likely date for the crucifixion of **Jesus Christ** in Jerusalem, AD30. He was put to death by order of Pontius Pilate, the Roman governor.

7 April 1906: Mt Vesuvius in Italy erupted. In nearby Naples, 100 people died as the weight of falling volcanic ash caused buildings to collapse.

Famous births...
William Kellogg, inventor of the breakfast cereal originally used in treating US mental patients. Born 1860.
Billie Holliday, jazz singer, born 1915.
Francis Xavier, Jesuit missionary, born in Spain, 1506.
David Low, World War 2 political cartoonist, born in New Zealand, 1891

APRIL 8

Today is **Pablo Picasso's** birthday. The great 20th century artist was born in 1881.

'Big Ben', the bell inside Westminster's clock tower, was cast on this day, 1858.

On 8 April 1546, the Roman Catholic Council of Trent declared that the Apocrypha formed part of the Bible.

On this day in 1939, King Zog of Albania fled his country as the Italians invaded on the eve of World War 2.

Some famous deaths...
Caracalla, the cruel Roman Emperor who murdered to get to the throne was himself assassinated, AD217.
El Greco, famous painter, died in Spain, 1614.
Elisha Graves Otis, who developed the first safety lift and spread the use of escalators. Died in New York, 1861.

On this day in 1865, the American Civil War came to an end. General Robert E Lee, commander of the Confederate (Southern) armies, surrendered to Ulysses S Grant at the Appomattox Courthouse.

9 April 1940: Without any warning, Hitler's troops launched a massive invasion of Denmark and Norway.

The Beatles split up on this day in 1970. Paul McCartney issued a writ in the High Court calling for the breaking up of their business partnership. The four were never to sing together again.

King Edward V came to the throne on 9 April 1483, at the age of 12. But he and his brother were not to last long. Richard III usurped Edward's throne and had the two princes locked in the Tower. They never emerged alive.

Winston Churchill was made an honorary US citizen on this day in 1963.

In 1942, William Temple was made the new Archbishop of Canterbury.

Today in 1838, London's National Gallery in Trafalgar Square was opened.

Isambard Kingdom Brunel, the famous Victorian engineer, was born in Portsmouth today in 1806. He built the first underwater tunnel, the Clifton Suspension Bridge, the Great Western Railway and three ocean-going liners.

Dietrich Bonhoeffer, the courageous German opponent of Hitler's regime, was hanged at the Flossenburg concentration camp on this day in 1945.

APRIL 10

10 April 1912: At noon, the RMS *Titanic* set sail on her maiden voyage from Southampton. One seaman was heard to say...

> God himself could not sink this ship.

It wasn't a good day to launch a ship, because today is a 'Dismal Day'. This day (and 23 others throughout the year) was considered unlucky in medieval times.

Today in 1939, Glen Miller and his band recorded *Little Brown Jug*.

Today's birthdays...
General William Booth, pioneering leader of the Salvation Army, born in Nottinghamshire, 1829. **Joseph Pulitzer**, journalist and newspaper owner, founder of the prestigious Pulitzer Prize. Born in Hungary, 1847.

APRIL 11

On this day in 1966, Frank Sinatra's *Strangers in the Night* was released in America.

A major archaeological discovery was announced this day in 1948. A shepherd boy, throwing stones into a cave by the Dead Sea had heard the sound of pottery breaking. He climbed into the cave to look and found a large number of jars stuffed full of ancient documents, 2,000 years old. They came to be known as the Dead Sea Scrolls.

On this day in 1689, William and Mary were crowned as King and Queen of Britain.

Meanwhile, Napoleon was sent into exile after he had abdicated as Emperor of France, today, 1814. He was sent to the Italian island of Elba.

Today in 1713, France gave Gibraltar to Britain. (They also threw in Newfoundland, Nova Scotia and Hudson Bay.)

APRIL 12

Today is Cosmonauts' Day in the USSR. This is because it is the anniversary of the first ever manned space flight. On 12 April 1961, 27-year-old Major Uri Gagarin was blasted into space, orbitted the Earth once and returned on a parachute. The news stunned the world - especially the Americans, who wanted to be the first to do it. His first impressions of the Earth from space?

The sky looks very very dark and the Earth bluish...

In ancient Rome, today was the festival of Ceres (the goddess of fertility). The celebrations lasted until 19th April.

The two rock'n'roll classics, *Rock Around the Clock* and *Shake, Rattle and Roll* were recorded in the same session by Bill Haley, this day in 1954.

The American Civil War began today in 1861, when the Southern army attacked Fort Sumter, Charleston. The war was fought chiefly because the Southern states wanted to maintain slavery.

Harry S Truman became US President on this day in 1945, on the death of President Franklin D Roosevelt.

APRIL 13

On this day in 1742, Handel's *Messiah* was first performed at The Music Hall in Fishamble Street, Dublin. Probably the most famous music in the Messiah is the 'Hallelujah Chorus'.

13 April 1970: On its outward flight to the Moon, an explosion in Apollo 13's Service Module crippled the spacecraft. With oxygen running low, the three astronauts had to retreat inside their lunar landing craft. Ninety hours and a trip around the Moon later, the astronauts made it back to Earth safely.

Today in 1848, Sicily gained its independence from Naples. Sicily is the largest island in the Mediterranean.

Today's birthday boys...
Thomas Jefferson, 3rd US President, and main author of the American *Declaration of Independence*. Born in 1743.
Richard Trevithick, developer of the steam engine. Born in Cornwall, 1771.
Samuel Beckett, Irish novelist and playwright, author of *Waiting for Godot*. Born 1906.

APRIL 14

14 April 1912: At 11.40pm the lookout on board the *Titanic* sighted an iceberg dead ahead of the ship. He rang three bells and telegraphed the ship's bridge, but it was too late. As the ship began to turn, the iceberg scraped down its side. The *Titanic* began to sink into the Atlantic.

14 April 1865: US President **Abraham Lincoln** and his wife went to a Washington theatre to see the new play *Our American Cousin*. Just after 10pm, an actor, John Wilkes Booth, crept into the president's box and shot him in the head. Booth jumped to the stage, breaking his leg,

but escaped for a few days until he was shot. Lincoln died the next morning.

There was also an attempted assassination of Tsar Alexander II on this day in 1879.

This day in 1360 was known as 'Black Monday' It was a day for the record books as far as the weather was concerned: One writer described it as... 'so full dark of mist and hail and so bitter cold that many men died on their horsebacks with the cold'.

Webster's Dictionary was first published on this day in 1828. It is famous for first laying down the American spellings of English words, like 'color', 'theater', etc.

Born on this day...
Sir John Gielgud, the actor who played the butler in *Arthur*. Born in London, 1904.
François Duvalier, murderous dictator of Haiti, known as 'Papa Doc'. Born 1907.
Rod Steiger, film actor, born in New York, 1925.
Anthony Perkins, the actor who starred in Hitchcock's *Psycho*. Born 1932.

Died on this day...
Richard Neville, the Earl of Warwick known as 'the Kingmaker' because of his political power. Died 1471.
George Frederick Handel, composer of *The Messiah*, died in London, 1759.

APRIL 15

15 April 1912: At 2.20am, only 2 hours 40 mins after striking an iceberg, the *Titanic* sank in the North Atlantic, with a loss of life in excess of 1,500. There had only been lifeboat space for 1,200 of the 2,200 passengers on board. The *Titanic* was on its maiden voyage to New York.

On this day in 1942, the island of Malta was awarded

the George Cross by King George VI. Malta had withstood over 2,000 air raids over four months, as Hitler tried to bomb the island into submission.

The Edict of Nantes, passed this day in 1598, granted religious toleration to Protestants living in Catholic France. Before this, Protestants had suffered severe persecution.

Staying with France, two famous French women died on this day...
Madame Tussaud, the skilfull French waxwork modeller, died at the grand old age of 90 in 1850.

Marquise de Pompadour, the mistress to Louis XV of France. She died at Versailles, 1764.

15 April 1797 saw the mutiny of the British Navy at Spithead. The sailors wanted an increase in wages. The mutiny ended peacefully when the Admiralty agreed to pay more.

Born today...
Sam Fox, outstanding model and singer. Born in 1966.
Jeffrey Archer, author of *Kane and Abel* and other novels. Born in 1940.
Henry James, the American novelist, was born today in 1843.

APRIL
16

The last battle to be fought on British soil took place on this day, 1746, at Culloden, in Scotland. The English, under William, Duke of Cumberland, defeated the Scottish, led by Charles Edward Stuart, the 'Young Pretender'. The Scots lost 2,500 men, killed during the battle and afterwards when they were pursued without mercy by the English troops.

The English lost 200 men. A £30,000 reward was put out for the Young Pretender, but he was never caught.

On this day in 1912, Miss Harriet Quimby became the first woman to fly the English Channel.

King Richard I ('Richard the Lion Heart') took a bath today in 1194, even though it wasn't his birthday. Richard was preparing himself for an important ceremony in Winchester. Baths (even for royalty) were very rare...

Lots of people chose today to be born:

Charlie Chaplin, the silent film comedian. Born in Kennington, London, 1889.
Sir Hans Sloane, whose library and museum started off the British Museum. Born 1660.
Charles Montagu, founder of the Bank of England. Born 1661.
Wilbur Wright, first man to fly in a heavier-than-air machine. Born 1867.
Peter Ustinov, film actor. Born 1921.
Kingsley Amis, author of books such as *Lucky Jim*. Born in London, 1922.
Gabriel Sabatini, Italian tennis star. Born in 1970.

And finally, the Roman Emperor **Marcus Salvius Otho** committed suicide on this day in the year AD69 at Brixellum. Just in case you hadn't heard.

APRIL 17

On this day in 1421, the sea broke through the dike at Dort, Holland. Over 100,000 people were drowned as the floodwaters surged across the countryside.

This day in 1961 also saw the Bay of Pigs fiasco, in Cuba. An American-backed invasion of Cuba was repulsed by Fidel Castro after three days.

On this day in 1969, Sirhan Sirhan, a Palestinian, was found guilty in Los Angeles of the murder of Robert Kennedy. He had shot Kennedy in a crowded hotel lobby. Sirhan was sentenced to the gas chamber.

Born today...
Edward Gibbon, author of *The Decline and Fall of the Roman Empire*, 1737.
Nikita Khrushchev, Soviet leader in the late 50s and early sixties. Born 1894.

Died today...
Benjamin Franklin, the American scientist and politician. He risked his life by flying a kite on a wire during a thunderstorm, to prove the difference between positive and negative electricity. Died 1790.

APRIL 18

18 April 1906: Measuring point 5 on the Richter Scale, a powerful earthquake struck San Francisco. 1,000 people were killed by collapsing buildings, and in the fire-storm that quickly followed the quake. Martial law was declared, and looters were shot in the streets.

Today in 1949, Eire was formally proclaimed a Republic.

On this day in 1689, the notorious **Judge Jeffreys** died in the Tower of London. Jeffreys was renowned for his cruel sentencing. After one English rebellion, he had 320 rebels executed and hundreds more flogged and exiled.

Today is the birthday of **Lucrezia Borgia**, the illegitimate daughter of a pope. Lucrezia was an aristocrat and a poisoner. She was born in Rome in 1480.

John Foxe, preacher and author of the best-selling *Foxe's Book of Martyrs,* died on this day in 1587. His book gave gruesome details of many of the executions for heresy during the reign of Queen 'Bloody' Mary.

APRIL 19

On the day in 1587, Sir Francis Drake 'singed the King of Spain's beard' by a daring attack on the Spanish port of Cadiz. In this one attack, Drake destroyed 10,000 tons of the Spanish Armada, delaying its attack on Britain by a year.

This day in 1775 saw the opening shots in the American War of Independence, at the town of Lexington. The American colonies were trying to break free from British rule. At Lexington, the British were defeated.

Today in 1912, literacy was made a condition for immigration into the United

States.

The Soviet Union launched the first unmanned space station, *Salyut,* on 19 April 1971.

The following gasped their last on this day...
George Gordon Byron, the romantic poet, died of a fever in Greece, 1824.

Benjamin Disraeli, British Prime Minister. Died 1881.
Charles Darwin, controversial scientist who proposed the theory of evolution. Died 1882. His parting words...

> I am not in the least afraid to die.

APRIL 20

20 April 753BC is the traditional date for the founding of the city of Rome by Romulus and Remus. Seven hundred years later, the Roman Empire stretched from the borders of Scotland to modern-day Iran.

On this day in 1889, a baby was born to an Austrian customs official and his wife at Braunau-am-Inn. Mr and Mrs Hitler decided to call their child **Adolf**.

Today is a 'Dismal Day'. This day (and 23 others throughout the year) was considered unlucky in medieval times.

Today in 1912, **Bram Stoker,** the author of Dracula, died in London. There were no bite-marks on his neck. Dracula the vampire is the most-portrayed horror character in film history.

On 20 April 1653, Oliver Cromwell dismissed Parliament, clearing the House of Commons with 30 soldiers. The Speaker was dragged down from his seat by his gown. Cromwell drove MPs out with the words...

> You are no Parliament. I say you are no Parliament. I will put an end to your sitting.

APRIL 21

On this day in 1918, the infamous **'Red Baron'** was shot down and killed during World War 1. Manfred von Richthofen, who had shot down 80 allied planes in less than two years, was named 'Red' because of his red Fokker triplane.

Today in 1972, the *Apollo 16* astronauts landed on the Moon.

Today is the birthday of three great women...
Catherine the Great, Empress of Russia, born in 1729.
Charlotte Brontë, novelist and author of *Jane Eyre*.

Born in Yorkshire, 1816.
Elizabeth II, Queen of the United Kingdom since 1952. Born in London, 1926.

21 April marks the death of:
King Henry VII, father of Henry VIII. Died in his palace in Richmond, 1509.
François Duvalier, the brutal dictator of Haiti, known as 'Papa Doc'. Died 1971.
Mark Twain, author of *Tom Sawyer* and *Huckleberry Finn*. He died in Connecticut in 1910, aged 74. He had once read an obituary for himself in a newspaper, and cabled the paper to say...

The report of my death was an exaggeration.

APRIL 22

After an 18-day voyage, the steamboat *Sirius* arrived in New York today in 1838, having crossed the Atlantic from Queenstown in Ireland. The *Sirius* was the first ship to cross under continuous steam power. They had to burn the furniture to

complete the crossing.

22 April 1707 saw the last sitting of the independent Scottish Parliament. After this date, Scotland and England were politically united.

On this day in 1073, Pope Gregory VII was enthroned in Rome. Gregory liked to throw his weight around. He once forced the Emperor of Germany, Henry IV, to stand for three days and nights barefoot in winter at the gate of Castle Canossa. Only then did he grant Henry forgiveness for demanding Gregory's abdication.

Today is the birthday of **Jack Nicholson**, the film actor. Nicholson starred in *One Flew Over the Cukoo's Nest* and many other movies. He was born in 1937.

Poison gas was used for the first time in warfare on this day in 1915. The new weapon was used by German forces on the Western front, during World War 1. Chemical weapons were first banned in 1925.

APRIL 23

Today is St George's Day. St George, although martyred in the Middle East, is the patron saint of England. His day has been celebrated in England since the Norman Conquest of 1066.

Today was a good day for Kings and Queens. King Charles II was crowned on this day in 1661, after 12 years spent in exile. The congregation in Westminster Abbey was showered with silver coins by the King's Treasurer. Meanwhile, Queen Anne, Charles's niece, was crowned today in 1702. Anne is the only English monarch who has had to be carried to her coronation. She was suffering from gout, and arrived at Westminster Abbey in a sedan chair, wearing a £12 wig.

Today is a sad day for literature. Two literary greats died on exactly the same day...
William Shakespeare, England's greatest dramatist, died today in 1616.
Miguel de Cervantes, Spanish author of Don Quixote, also died today in 1616.

As if that wasn't bad enough...
William Wordsworth, romantic poet, died today in 1850.

However, the good news is that **Roy Orbison** was born on this day in 1936.

On this day in 1930, Amy Johnson arrived in Darwin, Australia. She had flown solo from Britain in 19.5 days, piloting a second-hand Gipsy Moth. She was the first woman to make the journey.

The *Daily Express* was first published today in 1900.

Good news for kids: chocolate and sweet rationing ended in Britain after World War 2 on this day in 1949.

The Chinese launched their first satellite on 24 April 1970.

The Russian spacecraft *Soyuz 10* docked successfully with the space station *Salyut* on this day in 1971. *Salyut* was the first-ever space station, a 50ft cylinder in which cosmonauts lived for up to eight months before returning to Earth.

And now, some famous birthdays...
Edmund Cartwright, the inventor of the power-driven loom, one of the major inventions of the industrial revolution. Born in Nottinghamshire, 1743.
Anthony Trollope, the Victorian novelist who wrote *Barchester Towers* and others. Born in London, 1815.
Lord Haw Haw, British propagandist who worked for the Nazis. Born in New York, 1906.
Barbra Streisand, singer and film actress. Born in New York, 1942.

Today in 1731 saw the death of **Daniel Defoe**, the author of Robinson Crusoe.

Today is St Mark's Day. Mark is famous for writing Mark's Gospel, his version of the life of Jesus Christ. Mark's nickname was *kolobodaktulos*, a Greek word meaning 'stumpy-fingers'.

On this day in 1792, the guillotine was first used. Its victim was the French highwayman, **Monsieur Pelletier**, whose head rolled at the Place de Grève, Paris.

The German magazine *Stern* thought it had found the scoop of the century. On this day in 1983, *Stern* began to serialise the 'Hitler Diaries'. The 60-volumes were alleged to have been written by the Nazi leader himself. However, by early May, the scoop of the century had turned into the hoax of the century. The diaries had been cleverly faked by Konrad Kajau.

The head of the 'Little Mermaid' statue in Copenhagen harbour was sawn off and stolen today in 1964. The statue was in honour of the Danish children's author, Hans Christian Andersen.

Soviet and US troops finally met towards the end of World War 2 at the town of Torgau on the River Elbe. Ironically, the Torgau March was one of Hitler's favourite pieces of music!

Construction work began on the Suez Canal, today in 1859.

King Edward II was born today in 1284 at Caernarfon Castle, the son of Edward I. Baby Edward was the first English Prince of Wales. He was given this title as a diplomatic gesture to the recently-defeated Welsh. All male heirs to the throne since have been invested as Prince of Wales. Edward turned out to be brilliant at thatching cottages, but poor as a monarch.

APRIL 26

On this day in 1986, the nuclear reactor at Chernobyl exploded, causing a high radiation cloud to drift across Western Europe. The Chernobyl disaster was the worst ever nuclear reactor accident.

Madame Tussaud's new building in Marylebone Road, London, was opened today in 1928.

On this day in 1564, a baby boy was baptized in Stratford-upon-Avon. The name in the church register read: 'William Shaksper'.

Today's birthdays...
Rudolf Hess, Hitler's deputy, born in Alexandria, Egypt, in 1894.
Emma, Lady Hamilton, the daughter of a Cheshire blacksmith who eventually became Horatio Nelson's mistress. Born in 1765.

But I thought we were heading north!

APRIL 27

On this day in 1921, the Allies declared that Germany owed them £6,650m for World War 1. This bill was to cripple Germany and was one of the causes of the bitterness that led to World War 2.

On 27 April 1950, Britain formally recognized the State of Israel. Israel had come into existence almost two years earlier.

King David I came to the throne of Scotland on this day in 1124.

Born on this day...
Michael Fish, the BBC weatherman. Micahel was born in 1944.
Ulysses S Grant, commander of the Union Army in the American Civil War, he later became US President. Born this day in 1822.
Edward Whymper, the first man to reach the summit of

90

the Matterhorn. Born in London, 1840.

APRIL 28

C Day Lewis, Poet Laureate. Born in Sligo, Ireland, 1904.

On this day in 1789, the crew of HMS *Bounty* mutinied against their severe commander, Captain William Bligh. Bligh and 19 men were put into an open boat and cast adrift in the Pacific, while the mutineers took the Bounty to Tahiti. After an incredible 4,000-mile voyage, the boat reached Timor Island, Java. Six of the mutineers were condemned and three eventually hanged.

Today in 1940, Glen Miller and his band recorded *Pennsylvania 6-5000*. The title refers to the phone number of one of the band's girlfriend.

On 28 April 1923, Wembley's newly-built Empire Stadium had its first sporting event. Bolton Wanderers played West Ham for the FA Cup. The day nearly ended in disaster as the ground was allowed to fill to double its capacity. Bolton won the match 2-1.

Captain Cook first landed at Botany Bay in Australia today in 1770. Botany Bay is famous as the first prison colony in Australia. Cook named the newly-discovered continent New South Wales.

Benito Mussolini, the theatrical and brutal dictator of Italy during World War 2, came to a sticky end on this day in 1945. He was shot and strung up by his feet on a petrol station forecourt in Milan.

Born today: **Anthony Ashley Cooper** (also known as Lord Shaftesbury). Shaftesbury was one of the great Victorian reformers. He campaigned to reduce factory shifts to 10 hours a day, and to prevent women and children working in mines. He was born in London, 1801.

APRIL 29

This day was popularly believed in the middle ages to be the day when Noah & Co. left the ark after their one-year voyage.

On 29 April 1945, the German army in Italy, numbering almost a million troops, surrendered unconditionally to the Allies.

Born on this day...
William Randolph Hearst, newspaper magnate and basis for Orson Welles' film Citizen Kane. Born in San Francisco, 1863.
Sir Thomas Beecham, and **Sir Malcolm Sargent**, both orchestral conductors, born in 1879 and 1895.
Duke Ellington, jazz composer and pianist. Born in Washington DC, 1899.

Hirohito, Emperor of Japan from 1926 to 1988. Born in Tokyo, 1901.

Died on this day...
Alfred Hitchcock, film director and the master of suspense. Hitchcock directed some of the greatest spine-chilling, edge-of-your-seat films ever, including *Psycho*, and *The Birds*. He died of natural causes in 1980.
Wallace Carothers, the chemist who developed nylon, died in 1937.

APRIL 30

On this day in 1789, George Washington, heroic commander-in-chief of the American Revolutionary War, was inaugurated as first President of the United States.

This day in 1928 saw the start of the Flying Scotsman service.

30 April 1945: **Adolf Hitler** went to his room in the

bunker deep beneath the Chancellery building in Berlin. There he shot himself and died next to Eva Braun, whom he had married a few hours earlier. She killed herself with poison. It is estimated that Hitler caused the death of 30 million people in Europe.

Today in AD311, Christians were given legal recognition for the first time in the Roman Empire. The Edict of Nicomedia, issued by Galerius, allowed them to build meeting houses and worship as they liked, as long as they didn't disturb the peace.

Red Adair (the world-famous oil-platform fire-fighter of Texas) notched up another daredevil victory today in 1977. He successfully capped an oil rig fire on the Bravo Norwegian Ekofisk in the North Sea - a fire no one else could put out.

The South Vietnamese city of Saigon was renamed Ho Chi Minh City on this day, 1975.

APRIL QUIZ

1. *Dallas* was first screened on 2 April. Which member of the Royal Family has appeared on *Dallas*?
a) Prince Andrew
b) Prince Charles
c) Princess Margaret

2. The inventor of Morse Code died on 2 April. What is dash dash dash dash dot dash in Morse Code?
a) SOS
b) BBC
c) OK

3. What was the name of Dick Turpin's horse (he died on 7 April)?
a) Silver
b) Black Bess
c) Red Rum

4. What was Madame Tussaud's first name (she died 15 April)?
a) Claire
b) Claudette
c) Anne

5. Daniel Defoe, author of *Robinson Crusoe*, died on 24 April. Which of these is true about him?
a) he was put in the pillory
b) he was a desert island castaway
c) he was a dwarf

Answers on page 272

Name
May is named afer Maia, one of the
Roman gods. It is one of the four
months of the year named after gods
- the others being January (Janus),
March (Mars), and June (Juno).

Red Letter Days
• 1 May is May Day - the beginning of
summer, celebrated since before
Roman times
• 8 May is VE (Victory in Europe)
Day, marking the end of World War 2
in Europe in 1945
• 29 May is Restoration Day, when
the monarchy (under King Charles
II) was restored in Britain, 1660

MAY 1

Today is May Day, a public holiday in Britain. Since Roman times (and even before that), May 1st has been celebrated as the beginning of summer. The Romans dedicated the day to the goddess of fruit and flowers, Flora. In medieval England, Flora became the May Queen, a girl of the village who was crowned for the day. The villagers danced around a maypole, decorated local trees with flowers and did various other crazy things.

On this day in 1945, Russians forces captured Berlin, seven days before the end of World War 2 in Europe.

1 May 1960: An American U-2 plane flying over Russia was shot down by a ground-to-air missile. The Russians claimed it had flown over missile sites, taking spy photographs. The pilot, Francis Gary Powers, later pleaded guilty to espionage and was sentenced to 10 years in a Soviet prison.

On 1 May 1840, the first

'Penny Black' stamps were issued to the public.

The tallest and longest-standing maypole was lifted into place in the Strand, London, on this day in 1661. The 130-foot pole took 12 sailors four hours to lift, watched by a massive crowd and egged on by drums and trumpets. The maypole stood until 1717, when Sir Isaac Newton bought it to support a new telescope he had been given.

On the subject of tall objects, the Empire State Building (at 1,245 feet the world's tallest at the time) was opened by President Hoover on this day in 1931.

Today saw the world premiere of Orson Welles' film, *Citizen Kane*, in New York, 1941.

There's got to be an easier way to drill for oil!

MAY 2

2 May 1982: The Argentinian cruiser *General Belgrano* was sunk by torpedoes from a British submarine, the *Conqueror,* during the Falklands War. The sinking was controversial. Britain had warned Argentinian ships to stay out of a 200-mile exclusion zone, but even though the *Belgrano* was outside the zone and sailing away from it, the order was still given to fire.

Today's births include...
Bing Crosby, who crooned his first notes in Washington DC today in 1904.
Dr Benjamin Spock, the famous child-care specialist. His book told parents that they should let children do what they want, and sold 25 million copies. He was born in Connecticut, 1903.

Nancy Astor, Britain's first woman MP, died this day in 1964. Nancy Astor and Winston Churchill were natural enemies and often quarrelled with each other. For exmple...

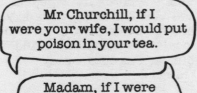

Mr Churchill, if I were your wife, I would put poison in your tea.

Madam, if I were your husband, I would drink that tea!

MAY 3

On this day in 1494, Christopher Columbus discovered the island of Jamaica. He was on his second expedition to the New World.

A duel with a difference took place near Paris today in 1808. Monsieur de Granpré and Monsieur Le Pique fought a bitter duel high above the ground in balloons. Fortunately, the shots missed the balloons themselves, but unfortunately one of them found Monsieur Le Pique, who was killed.

On 3 May in the year AD326, St Helena (mother of the

Roman Emperor) reported that she had discovered the cross on which Christ was crucified in Jerusalem. The cross, complete with nails, was supposedly discovered in an old underground cistern.

Today is a 'Dismal Day'. In medieval times, this day (along with 23 others throughout the year) was considered unlucky.

Pete Seeger, the American folk singer who wrote *Where Have all the Flowers Gone?* was born in New York on this day in 1919.

On 4 May 1979, Margaret Thatcher became Britain's first woman Prime Minister.

The first Exocet missile was fired in anger on this day in 1982. It was fired from an Argentinian aircraft during the Falklands War, and its target was HMS *Sheffield*. The *Sheffield* received a direct hit and sank with the loss of 21 lives.

Waltzing Matilda officially became Australia's national anthem today in 1976.

This day saw the founding of two important companies. The Cunard Company came into being in 1839, and became known later in the century for its transatlantic liners. Meanwhile, Charlie

Rolls and Fred Royce got together in 1904 to form a little car company.

The Derby, England's foremost horse race, was first run today in 1780. The Derby is named after the 12th Earl of Derby, who first had the idea.

On this day in 1970, four students were shot dead and 11 others injured at the Kent State University, USA. The students were protesting against the Vietnam War when National Guard troops fired into the crowd. Two of the students were women, and all four were unarmed.

MAY 5

5 May 1980: Wearing black uniforms and balaclavas, the SAS stormed the terrorist-held Iranian Embassy in London. Nineteen hostages had been held there for six days, and the terrorists had just killed a hostage with the threat of killing one more every 30 minutes. Only one terrorist survived the SAS attack.

America launched its first man into space today in 1961. Alan Shepard completed a 15-minute sub-orbital flight that took him 115 miles high. Due to a four-hour delay before launch, Shepard had to relieve his bladder into his spacesuit. No one had thought of installing a loo in the capsule...

Today's birthdays...
Søren Kierkegaard, famous Danish philosopher, born in 1813.
Karl Marx, founder of Marxism, born in 1818.

Napoleon Bonaparte died in exile on the island of St Helena on this day in 1821. Some claim that he was murdered.

MAY 6

6 May 1937: The German airship *Hindenburg* burst into flames as it landed at Lakenhurst, New Jersey. Within 32 seconds, 35 people had died as the ship's seven million cubic feet of hydrogen became a ball of fire. Erich Spehl, an airship worker, was suspected of causing the fire using a camera flashbulb and torch battery, set to go off using a pocket watch. Miraculously one or two people stepped off the *Hindenburg* completely unsinged.

On this day in 1954, Roger Bannister, a medical student, ran the first four-minute mile at Oxford. He covered 1 mile in 3 minutes 59.4 seconds.

The island of Manhattan (now part of New York City) was bought from the Indians by Peter Minuit for a few trinkets, on this date in 1626. Manhattan is worth considerably more today.

6 May was a birthday for...
Rudolph Valentino, the glamorous film star of the 1920s. Born in Italy, 1895. **Czar Nicholas II** of Russia, the last czar. Born in 1868. **Sigmund Freud**, the father of psychoanalysis. Born in 1856.

MAY 7

On 7 May 1928, women were given the same voting status as men for the first time. The voting age for women was dropped from 30 to 21.

7 May 1915: At 2.12pm, a Cunard liner, the *Lusitania*, was hit by two torpedoes fired by a German submarine. The ship was only eight miles off the coast of Ireland, on its voyage from New York to Liverpool. Nearly 1,200 passengers drowned (some of them American) as the ship sank in 21 minutes. This outrage helped to draw America into World War 1.

On this day in 1908, the first Old Age Pension was legislated in the UK. The over-70s were to get 5 shillings (25p) a week - but only if they were earning less than £31 10 shillings per year. In the first six months, over 800,000 people applied for the pension.

Born on this day...
Robert Browning, poet and writer, London 1812.
Johannes Brahms, classical composer, Hamburg 1833.
Edwin Herbert Land, inventor of polaroid cameras, Connecticut 1909.
Gary Cooper, film star, Montana 1901.

Today is celebrated as VE Day in Britain. Victory in Europe was achieved on this day in 1945 as the German armed forces surrendered unconditionally to the Allies. American and Soviet generals received the surrender from General Jodl in a small school in Rheims.

Today's birthdays...
Gary Glitter, 1970s pop star. Gary was born in 1944.
Harry S Truman, President of the US and the first (and so far the only) person to order the use of nuclear weapons in wartime. Born in 1884.

Sweden abolished capital

On this day in 1885, Sarah Ann Henley attempted to commit suicide by leaping from the Clifton Suspension Bridge, Bristol. However, her skirt and petticoat acted as a parachute, slowing her fall. She landed in the mud of the River Avon, escaping only with bruises and a set of ruined clothes.

On this day in 1969, Pope Paul VI ordered that a number of popular saints should be deleted from the church's calendar. **St Catherine** (of Catherine-Wheel fame), **St Christopher** (pictured on charms hung up in cars) and 30 other saints

were made unemployed. **St Nicholas** (Santa Claus) and **St George** (of England) were made optional saints.

Today in 1671, Colonel Thomas Blood, an Irish adventurer, attempted to steal the crown jewels from the Tower of London. He would only confess what he had done to King Charles himself.

London's Piccadilly Circus was first lit by electricity, this day in 1932.

The first flight over the North Pole took place today in 1926. Richard Byrd and Floyd Bennett, two American aviators, performed their fly-past during a 16-hour flight from Norway.

Today in 1945 was Liberation Day for the Channel Islands. The Germans had occupied the islands for just under five years, during World War 2.

Sir James Barrie, the author of *Peter Pan*, was born in Scotland on this day in 1860.

MAY 10

10 May 1941: Rudolf Hess, Hitler's deputy, got into a plane and flew from Germany to Britain on a secret 'peace mission'. He parachuted into Scotland, and broke his ankle on landing near a crofter's cottage. Hitler was furious at Hess's action, the British were puzzled, and Hess ended up in the Tower of London. He was later moved to Spandau Prison and remained there until his death 46 years later in 1987.

The final rails were laid today in 1869 joining America's Central Pacific and Union Pacific Railways. For the first time, trains were now able to run from the east coast right across the continent to the west. The final link was made at Promontory, in Utah.

On this day in 1940, two events took place in World War 2...
Winston Churchill was made Prime Minister and took charge of Britain's war effort.
The Home Guard or 'Dad's Army', as they were known, was established. Men too old for the armed forces were used for local defence, especially on Britain's exposed southern coast.

Today's birthdays...
Bono, lead singer of U2. Born today in 1960.
Fred Astaire, who tap-danced his way across many Hollywood films, was born this day in 1899.

MAY 11

On this day in 1941, London suffered one of the worst bombing raids of World War 2. During the raid, the chamber of the House of Commons was destroyed.

11 May 1985: During the first half of a football match between Bradford City and Lincoln, fire broke out in the main stand of Bradford's home ground. In seconds, the wooden stand was a mass of flames, engulfing the spectators. Over 40 fans died in the blaze.

Today marks the birthday of the original 'Siamese' twins. **Chang and Eng Bunker** were born in Siam (Thailand) in 1811, and were joined at the chest. They went on to marry two American women and to have between them 22 children.

On this day in 1949, Siam was given a new name: Thailand.

Spencer Perceval, the Prime Minister, was assassinated on this day in 1812. His assassin, John Bellingham, coolly shot him as he was entering the lobby of the House of Commons. Only one week later Bellingham was hanged.

Salvador Dali, bizarre Spanish artist, was born this day in 1904.

MAY 12

On this day in 1926, the General Strike ended in Britain. The strike, which had involved all of Britain's essential services, was the first in British history. It had started at midnight on 3 May.

12 May 1937 was Coronation Day for King George VI. George had never expected to become king, but was suddenly pushed forward when his older brother, Edward VIII, abdicated to marry a divorced woman. George VI's queen is the present Queen Mother.

The Berlin Blockade was

lifted today in 1949. The blockade on all food and supplies had been imposed by the Soviet Union, whose territory surrounded the city. For almost a year, British and American planes had flown in 2,500 tons of food a day to help the isolated city.

Born on this day...
Florence Nightingale was born today in 1820. Florence (named after the Italian city where she was born) revolutionized British nursing in the way she ran her hospital during the Crimean War. She managed to reduce the death rate among wounded troops from 42 per cent to 2 per cent.

Edward Lear, the man who popularized limericks in Britain, was born in London in 1812. This is a limerick that he *didn't* write...

A Radio One DJ called Sime,
Thought history was really
*   sublime,*
He talked about dates
To all his best mates,
Till they grabbed him and
*   chucked him in slime.*

MAY 13

13 May 1981: Pope John Paul II was shot as he rode in the popemobile through the crowds in St Peter's Square, Rome. The 23-year-old Turkish gunman, Mehmet Ali Agca, was almost lynched by the crowd. The pope made a full recovery, and later visited Agca in prison to forgive him.

On this day in 1940, Winston Churchill gave his inspiring 'Blood, toil, tears and sweat' speech in Parliament after becoming Prime Minister.

Faced with the menace of Nazi Germany, he said...

I have nothing to offer but blood, toil, tears and sweat.

Born today...
Stevie Wonder, pianist and singer. Born in 1950
Peter Gabriel, rock musician, born on exactly the same day, 1950.
Joe Louis, the longest-reigning world heavyweight boxing champion. Joe was born in Alabama in 1914.
Maria Theresa, Empress of Austria, born in Vienna 1717.

MAY 14

On 14 May 1650, the British Parliament voted in favour of capital punishment for adultery. However, this law was never carried out on anyone.

Samuel Morse transmitted his first morse code message on the US telegraph, today in 1844.

Today's birthday boys... **Dante Alighieri**, the Italian poet who wrote the *Inferno*, was born in 1265.

Eric Morecambe, of the comic duo Morecambe and Wise, was born in 1926. (His real surname was Bartholomew, but he named himself after Morecambe Bay.)

Gabriel Fahrenheit, the Polish physicist who first used mercury in thermometers. Born in 1686.

MAY 15

On this day in 1948, Israel declared itself to be an independent state. Immediately, five Arab states invaded the country, but the war ended with Israel gaining even more territory. For the first time since AD70, the Jewish people had a land of their own.

This day sees three firsts... The **first electric tram service** was opened in London by King Edward VII, on this day in 1903.

The world's **first regular airmail service** was started in the US today in 1918. The mail was flown between New York and Washington.

The **first broadcast quiz programme** was made in Canada, 15 May 1935.

On this day in 1800, James Hatfield attempted to assassinate King George III.

US astronaut Gordon Cooper orbitted the Earth 22 times on this day in 1963. On his final orbits, several electrical systems in his capsule failed, but Gordon remained icy cool and piloted the capsule down to a perfect splashdown in the Pacific.

16 May 1900: After a seven-month siege during the South African Boer War, the town of Mafeking was saved on this day by the arrival of British troops. Colonel Baden-Powell (who later founded the Boy Scouts) had held off the Dutch Boer army who were trying to capture the town. This event, known as 'the Relief of Mafeking' caused great celebration when the news reached Britain.

Today in 1969, the Soviet spacecraft *Venus 5* landed on the surface of Venus. Venus didn't exactly lay on a red-carpet welcome. The ground temperature at the time was 480°C, and it was raining sulphuric acid...

On 16 May 1929, the first Academy awards for film were presented in Los Angeles. It was two more years before the awards were nicknamed 'oscars'.

Talking of Hollywood, here are a couple of birthdays... **Bob Hope**, the US comedian, was born in Britain today in 1905. Bob was taken to America when he was two. **Liberace**, the flamboyant pianist and wearer of exotic fur coats. Born in Wisconsin, 1919.

MAY 17

17 May 1943 was an eventful night at the mighty Möhne and Eder dams in Germany. Both dams, which supplied vital energy to sustain Germany's war effort, were destroyed by top-secret British bombs dropped by the Dambusters Squadron. The bombs, designed by the engineer Barnes Wallis, bounced across the water behind the dams until they exoloded against the dam wall.

On this day in 1916, the Daylight Saving Act was passed by Parliament. It introduced the idea of putting the clocks forward by one hour in spring, and back one hour in the autumn, to make best use of daylight and reduce coal bills. Four days later, British clocks were put forward for the first time.

Born today...
Edward Jenner, the discoverer of vaccination. Born in Berkeley, Gloucestershire, 1749.
Sir Norman Lockyer, the man who discovered helium, was born in 1836.

MAY 18

On this day in 1888, the first horizontal disc record, developed by Emile Berliner, was demonstrated to the public. Before this time, records had been cylindrical.

On 18 May 1982, the Revd Sun Myung Moon, the leader of the Unification Church (the sect known as 'the Moonies'), was found guilty in the US of tax-dodging.

Napoleon was declared Emperor of France on this day in 1804.

Today in 1642 saw the founding of the city of Montreal, in Canada. Its original name was *Ville Marie*.

MAY 19

19 May 1980: At 8.39am, the top third of Mt St Helens in Washington State, USA, was blown apart by a massive volcanic eruption. The eruption turned the nearby River Toutle into a torrent of mud, killing eight people.

Anne Boleyn, Henry VIII's second wife, was beheaded at the Tower of London before a large crowd, this day in 1536. Henry, as a friendly gesture, had an expert executioner brought over from France to do the job with a sword, rather than using the more messy axe. He hid his sword under a bale of hay until the last second. He then distracted her attention and sliced off her head before she knew it. Anne's final words...

> The executioner is, I believe, an expert ... and my neck is very slender. Oh God, have pity on my soul!

On this day in 1588, the Spanish Armada set sail from Lisbon, destination England, ruled by Queen Elizabeth I (the daughter of Anne Boleyn).

At 6.15am on 19 May 1897, Oscar Wilde was released from Pentonville Prison, London, after serving two years hard labour for homosexuality. The sentence broke his health. Three years later, at the age of 46, he died.

Died on this day...
William Gladstone, four times Prime Minister of Britain. He was disliked by Queen Victoria, but introduced voting by secret ballot. Died in 1898.
TE Lawrence, known as 'Lawrence of Arabia'. He led the Arabs into an uprising against Turkish rule between 1916 and 1918. Lawrence was killed in Britain in a motorbike accident, 1935.

107

MAY 20

On this day in 1910, Halley's Comet passed within 13 million miles of the Earth. Halley's Comet is the brightest of the regular comets circling the Sun, visiting our region of space once every 76 years.

On 20 May 1892, the last broad gauge train, pulled by *The Cornishman*, left Paddington Station on its final run to Penzance. The broad gauge (where the rails were seven feet apart) came to an end through an act of Parliament, losing out to the standard gauge of 4 feet 8.5 inches.

A partial eclipse of the Sun was seen in Britain on this day in 1966.

Christopher Columbus, the Italian who went on voyages of exploration for the King of Portugal, died in Spain, today in 1506. Despite his great voyages of discovery, Columbus died in poverty.

On this day in 1501, the Portuguese discovered Ascension Island. The island is an ancient volcano with its peak just above the surface of the Atlantic Ocean.

On 20 May 1939, regular commercial flights began between the United States and Europe. The company running them was called Pan-American Airways.

Today's baby boys...
William George Fargo, the founding partner of Wells-Fargo, the US coach service. Bill was born in New York, 1818.
Moshe Dayan, the Israeli general and politician who wore an eye patch. Moshe was born in Palestine, 1915.

On this day in 1927, Captain Charles Lindbergh made the first solo flight across the Atlantic in his plane *Spirit of St Louis*. He set out on his 33-hour flight on 20 May from New York and landed in Paris at 10.21pm.

Today in 1910 saw the funeral of King Edward VIII. His nephew, the German Emperor Wilhelm II, was furious. In the funeral procession, he was upstaged by a dog. The place immediately behind the coffin, normally reserved for the chief mourner, was kept for the King's fox terrier, 'Caesar'.

On this day in 1553, Lady Jane Grey was forced for political reasons to marry Lord Guildford Dudley. She reluctantly became queen a few weeks later, on 9 July, but was forced off the throne by Queen Mary after only 10 days, and executed.

The Manchester Ship Canal was officially opened on this day in 1894.

King Henry VI was murdered today in 1471.

Today's birthdays...
Albrecht Dürer, 1471. Albrecht was a famous picture engraver.
King Philip II of Spain, 1527. Phil wanted to marry Queen Elizabeth I, but he ended up sending the Spanish Armada against her instead.
Duke of Bridgewater, 1736. The Duke pioneered canal-building in Britain.
Elizabeth Fry, 1780. Elizabeth was one of the first prison reformers.

MAY 22

22 May 1960: On the coast of Chile, the sea suddenly started to retreat until it was out of sight. It went down far below the low tide mark, revealing old wrecks and stranded fish. Twenty minutes later, the water returned as a 26-foot wave travelling at 125mph. Houses all along the coast were smashed and thousands lost their lives.

On this day in 1900, the age limit for boys working in mines was raised from 12 to 13.

Whipsnade Zoo opened its gates to the public, today in 1931.

This day in 1961 saw the installation of the Post Office's new public telephones. Instead of pressing buttons A or B (as in the old phone boxes) you now simply pushed your money into the slot when the pips sounded.

London's Blackwall Tunnel was opened by the Prince and Princess of Wales, today in 1897.

Three authors are remembered today...
Hergé, the creator of the cartoon character Tintin, was born in 1907.
Arthur Conan Doyle, author of the Sherlock Holmes books, was born in 1859.
Victor Hugo, French author of *Les Misérables* and other novels, died this day, 1885.

This day is also a birthday for former footballer **George Best**. George was born in 1946.

MAY 23

On this day in 1934, the US bank robbers **Bonnie and Clyde** were mown down in a police ambush in Louisiana. They had killed 12 people, and were caught in a hail of 50 bullets.

Captain Kidd was hanged for piracy on this day in 1701, along with three partners in crime. Kidd had been promised a free pardon if he gave himself up, but he was double-crossed by the British. His final words...

> This is a very false and faithless generation.

Henry VIII divorced his wife Catherine of Aragon on this day in 1533. It was his first divorce. He soon developed a taste for it.

Born today...
Sir Charles Barry, the architect who rebuilt the Houses of Parliament in the 1860s. Born in London, 1795.

Died today...
Heinrich Himmler, the head of the SS and Gestapo in Nazi Germany. He committed suicide after he was captured in 1945.

MAY 24

On this day in 1930, Amy Johnson arrived in Australia after the first female solo flight from London. Her 10,000-mile flight took just over 19 days. At one point she had to use sticking-plasters to repair her wings.

On 24 May 1968, the Rolling Stones' *Jumpin' Jack Flash* was released.

Dartmoor Prison received its first inmates today in 1809.

On this day in 1929, the Marx Brothers' first movie opened in New York - *The Cocoanuts*. The Marx Brothers hated it and wanted to destroy it, but the movie was a great box-office success and made over $2 million in just two months.

The Brooklyn Bridge in New York was opened on this day in 1883.

Queen Victoria shares her birthday with **Bob Dylan** today. Victoria was born in Kensington Palace in 1819. Bob was born as Robert Zimmerman in Minnesota, 1941.

MAY 25

Today is a 'Dismal Day'. In medieval times, this day (along with 23 others throughout the year) was considered unlucky.

The first-ever woman barrister in Britain qualified on this day in 1921.

On 25 May 1768, Captain Cook set sail on his first voyage of discovery. Cook is famous for his explorations in the Pacific and along the east coast of Australia.

Coventry Cathedral was rededicated today in 1962, after its destruction by German bombs during World War 2.

Born on this day...
Lord Beaverbrook, newspaper giant, 1879.
Igor Ivanovich Sikorsky, inventor and helicopter builder, Kiev 1889.

MAY 26

Today is the feast day of St Augustine, first Archbishop of Canterbury.

Michael Barrett was the last person in England to be publicly executed when he went to the scaffold before a large crowd at 8am on this day in 1868. He was hanged outside Newgate Prison in London for a bombing which killed 12 people.

On this day in 1923, the first 24-hour Le Mans Grand Prix was run.

On 26 May 1828, 16-year-old Kaspar Hauser, known as 'the Wild Boy' was found in rags wandering the market-place at Nuremberg, Germany. He claimed that he had been kept locked up in a small cupboard from his earliest memory, in a space where he could not even stand up. The truth of his claims was never proved.

Today's births...
George Formby, Lancashire, ukulele-playing comedian, famous for his song *Cleaning Windows*. George was born in 1904.
John Wayne, the star of Western films. John was born in 1907. His real name was Marion Morrison. Can you imagine a cowboy called Marion?

MAY 27

The English habeas corpus Act was first passed by Parliament today in 1679. *Habeas corpus* is Latin for 'have the body', and the law forced the keepers of prisoners to declare in court why the prisoner was being detained. Although habeas corpus is fundamental to English law, it has often been repealed in times of national emergency.

San Francisco's Golden Gate Bridge was opened on this day in 1937. The bridge across San Francisco Bay spans a 4,200-foot gap.

27 May 1941: After a three-day pursuit by Royal Navy ships, the German battleship *Bismarck* was shelled, bombed, torpedoed and finally sunk.

King John came to the English throne on this day in 1199. John was the younger brother of Richard the Lion Heart, who had just died. He had tried to steal the crown from Richard a number of times before.

Born on this day were...
Cilla Black, 60s singer and 80s presenter of Blind Date. Born in 1943.
Henry Kissinger, President Nixon's Secretary of State. Born in 1923.

MAY 28

On this day in 1931, Swiss Professor Auguste Picard and scientist Charles Kipfer became the first men to travel through the stratosphere, which begins 6 miles (10 kilometres) above the Earth. Their balloon achieved 52,462 feet.

On this day in 1967, Francis Chichester arrived back in Plymouth in his yacht *Gipsy Moth IV* after the first solo round-the-world voyage. It had taken him 119 days.

On 28 May 1987, 19-year-old Mathias Rust flew through a hole in Russia's air defences to land his Cessna plane in Red Square, Moscow. He signed autographs for the curious onlookers before he was arrested and led away.

Today's birthdays include...
Dr Joseph Guillotin, who refined the French guillotine so that it would provide instantaneous death. Born 1738.
William Pitt the Younger, became Britain's youngest-ever Prime Minister at the age of 24. Born 1759.
Ian Fleming, author of the James Bond books. Born 1908.

MAY 29

Edmund Hillary and his sherpa, Norgay Tenzing, were the first men to stand on the summit of Mt Everest. They reached the Earth's highest point at 11.30am on this day in 1953.

29 May 1985: At the European Cup Final, Liverpool football fans rioted in the stands of the Heysal Stadium in Brussels. In the panic, 41 Italian and Belgian supporters were trampled or crushed to death as a wall collapsed.

On this day in 1660, King Charles II entered London amidst great rejoicing. He had returned to London from

Holland, after 11 years in exile following the execution of his father, Charles I. It was Charles' 30th birthday

On 29 May 1942, Bing Crosby went into a recording studio and sang *White Christmas*. By December 1961 20 million copies had sold, earning it a platinum disc as the world's best seller at the time. By 1970, 30 million copies had been sold.

A new radio series, *The Archers*, had its first broadcast today in 1950.

MAY 30

On this day in 1431, **Joan of Arc** was burnt as a witch by the English at Rouen. She believed that she had been called by God to expel the English from France - and was successful in a number of battles against them.

Joan of Arc was declared a saint by Pope Benedict XV, on this day in 1920.

On 30 May 1536, Henry VIII married his third wife, Jane Seymour, in private. Only 11 days earlier, wife no.2, Anne Boleyn, had been executed.

Queen Victoria was almost assassinated by John Francis today in 1842.

On this day in 1959, the first hovercraft flight took place at Cowes, Isle of Wight. The hovercraft weighed in at four tons.

Peter the Great, the Tsar of Russia, was born today in 1672.
WS Gilbert (of Gilbert &

115

MAY 31

On this day in 1911, the RMS *Titanic* was launched in Belfast.

Today's birthdays...
Clint Eastwood, mean cowboy in numerous spaghetti westerns, was born today in 1930.
Terry Waite, Special Envoy for the Archbishop of Canterbury. Born in 1939.

31 May 1962: The Nazi SS officer **Adolf Eichmann** was hanged in Israel for his war crimes. Eichmann, who took part in the 'final solution' against the Jews, escaped to Argentina after Germany fell in 1945. He was captured and brought to Israel by Israeli secret agents.

The Girl Guides were founded on this day in 1910.

On this day in 1553, Anne Boleyn was crowned Henry VIII's second queen at Westminster Abbey. But the crowds lining the coronation route were sullen and quiet. Anne was unpopular.

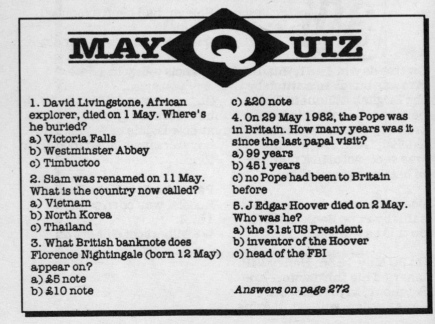

MAY QUIZ

1. David Livingstone, African explorer, died on 1 May. Where's he buried?
a) Victoria Falls
b) Westminster Abbey
c) Timbuctoo

2. Siam was renamed on 11 May. What is the country now called?
a) Vietnam
b) North Korea
c) Thailand

3. What British banknote does Florence Nightingale (born 12 May) appear on?
a) £5 note
b) £10 note
c) £20 note

4. On 29 May 1982, the Pope was in Britain. How many years was it since the last papal visit?
a) 99 years
b) 451 years
c) no Pope had been to Britain before

5. J Edgar Hoover died on 2 May. Who was he?
a) the 31st US President
b) inventor of the Hoover
c) head of the FBI

Answers on page 272

June

Name
June is named after the Roman goddess Juno. Juno was married to Jupiter, the father of all the Roman gods. She was associated with women, the moon and with hunting.

Red Letter Days
• 6 June is D-Day, marking the events of this day in 1944, during World War 2
• 18 June is Waterloo Day, celebrating the Battle of Waterloo, fought in 1805
• 21 June is the Summer Solstice
• 24 June is Midsummer's Day

JUNE 1

Today in 1915 saw the first bomb attack on London by German Zeppelins, during World War 1. This was the first time ever that London had been threatened from the air.

The LP *Sgt. Pepper's Lonely Hearts Club Band* was released by the Beatles on this day in 1967.

Bob Dylan shocked and horrified his folk fans this evening, 1966, at the Royal Albert Hall by playing an electric guitar. Up until this point, Bob had been an acoustic guitar-strumming folk musician.

On this day in 1939 a new submarine, the *Thetis,* sank in Liverpool Bay during trials. The stern of the submarine surfaced and four crew members managed to escape through a hatch. After three days, the bow end of the submarine was brought to the surface, allowing only six more men out. The *Thetis* then sank for good. Ninety-nine men were lost.

On 1 June 1957, ERNIE selected its first premium bond prize-winners.

Marilyn Monroe, named Norma Jean Baker, was born in California, today in 1926.

JUNE 2

On this day in 1953, Queen Elizabeth II was crowned in Westminster Abbey. Typically, it tipped down with rain. For the first time ever, the coronation of an English monarch was seen around the world on television.

The US craft *Surveyor 1* soft-landed on the Moon today in 1966. *Surveyor 1* sent back to Earth the first colour pictures of the lunar surface.

The Gordon Riots broke out in London on this day in 1780. The riots were against Roman Catholics, and lasted for over a week.

The following people were

born on this day…
Jesse Boot, born in 1850. Never heard of him? Jesse was the founder of Boots the Chemist.

Sir Edward Elgar, the English classical composer who wrote the music of *Land of Hope and Glory*. Born 1857.

JUNE 3

The Battle of Midway commenced on this day in 1942. US and Japanese aircraft carriers and warships clashed at the island of Midway in the Pacific. The Japanese were forced to retreat, marking a turning point in World War 2.

The Duke of Windsor married Mrs Wallis Simpson in France, on this day in 1937. The Duke (formerly King Edward VIII) had been forced to give up his throne to marry, because Mrs Simpson was a divorcee.

On 3 June 1956, British Rail abolished 3rd Class on their trains.

On this day in 1665, the Duke of York defeated the Dutch fleet off the coast of Harwich. The two nations were at war partly because the English had captured the Dutch town of New Amsterdam, renaming it 'New York'.

The US spacecraft *Gemini 9*, with two astronauts on board, was launched today in 1966.

King George V was born today in 1865.
Jefferson Davis, president of the southern states of America during the Civil War, was born on this day, 1808. His birthday is still celebrated in some southern American states.
Franz Kafka, the novelist who wrote the nightmarish *The Trial*, died today in 1924.

JUNE 4

4 June 1913: **Emily Davison**, a suffragette, tried to grab the reins of the King's horse as it galloped past her at the Derby. She fell beneath the horse and was fatally injured, dying 10 days later.

On this day in 1940, the evacuation of 338,226 British and French troops was completed at Dunkirk. Hitler's armies had cornered the Allied troops, but 1,200 British vessels (many of them pleasure boats) crossed the English Channel to rescue them. The evacuation had begun on 29 May and was the greatest evacuation in military history.

Today in 1784 saw the first flying woman and the first flying opera singer. Madame Thible, who was both a woman and an opera singer ascended in a French hot-air balloon. Did she generate her own air?

King George III was born at 7.30am in London, today in 1738.

JUNE 5

5 June 1783: Joseph and Étienne Montgolfier made the first flight in human history, when their hot-air balloon suddenly took off, much to their surprise and the surprise of the villagers of Annonay, France, who were watching. The balloon was powered by burning straw and wool, and rose to about 6,000 feet before descending.

On this day in 1967, the Israeli Six-Day War started when Israel launched an air attack against Egypt and Jordan. The war ended on 10 June, after Israel had captured the whole of Jerusalem.

Bobby Kennedy, brother of John Kennedy, was assassinated in the lobby of a

Los Angeles hotel. He and his supporters were just celebrating his victory in the Californian Democratic Primary, when a Palestinian stepped forward and shot him at point-blank range. Many were sure that Kennedy would become the next US president. He died the following day.

Lord Kitchener died on this day in 1916. Kitchener's face appeared on the famous World War 1 poster, with the slogan: 'Your country needs YOU.' He died when his ship, travelling to Russia, sank after hitting a mine off the Orkneys.

JUNE 6

Today was D-Day in 1944. At around 5am, the Allied armies landed on the beaches of German-occupied Normandy and began to fight their way inland. Within three months, Paris was liberated. It was the beginning of the end of World War 2.

The world's first drive-in cinema was opened in Camden, New Jersey, on this day in 1933. There were 10 acres for the cars to park.

Today in 1966 saw the first screening on BBC television of *Til Death Us Do Part*, starring Warren Mitchell as Alf Garnett.

Born on this day...

Bjorn Borg, five-times winner of Wimbledon. Bjorn in 1956.
Diego Velasquez, famous Spanish artist. Born in Seville, 1599.
Robert Falcon Scott, born in Devon, 1868. Scott was the first Briton to reach the South Pole (in 1912). His party never made it back through the snow. His last note, discovered later, said...

Had we lived, I should have had a tale to tell.

Died on this day...
Carl Gustav Jung, brilliant psychologist. Died in Switzerland, 1961.
John Paul Getty, widely hailed as the richest man in the world. Died in 1976.
Louis Chevrolet, US car designer. Died 1941.

On 7 June 1665, the Great Plague was first reported in London. Samuel Pepys, the famous diarist, writing about the hottest day he had ever known, saw red crosses marked on doors in the capital, showing that there were cases of plague inside. Within days, whole streets were full of doors with red crosses.

On this day in 1967, Israeli paratroopers captured the Wailing Wall in Jerusalem during the Six Day War. A near-riot broke out that evening as thousands of Jews made their way to the wall, the holiest site in Judaism. For the first time in 1,900 years, Jerusalem belonged to the Jewish people.

King James I dissolved the 'Addled' Parliament on this day in 1614. The Parliament had only sat for two months, passed no acts and argued non-stop with the king.

On this day in 1906, the Cunard liner *Lusitania* was launched. Nine years later, during World War 1, the *Lusitania* was sunk by a German torpedo, with the loss of 1,200 lives.

The next transit of Venus across the face of the Sun will take place on this day in 2004.

Today is a birthday for the rock singer **Prince**. He was born this day in 1960.

Died today...
EM Forster, author of *A Room with a View* and *A Passage to India*, 1970.
Muhammad, the founder of Islam, AD 632.

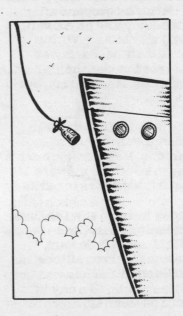

JUNE 8

On this day in 1968, James Earl Ray was detained at Heathrow Airport and arrested for the murder of Martin Luther King, the American civil rights leader, on 4 April. King had been gunned down as he stood on the balcony of his motel.

The first flight between the US and Australia took place on this day in 1928. Charles Kingsford-Smith and Captain TP Ulm flew from Oakland, California, on 31 May, arriving in Brisbane after island-hopping on Hawaii and Fiji.

Two royals died on this day... **Hardicanute**, King of England and son of King Canute, he died 1042. **The Black Prince** (the son of King Edward III). He was called the Black Prince because his armour was this colour. Died in 1376.

JUNE 9

Not much happened on this day in history. But there was at least one birth and one death...

George Stephenson was born in Newcastle, this day in 1781. George is known to history as the man who built the first commercially successful steam engine. His most famous engine was the *Rocket*.

Charles Dickens died on this day, 1870. Charlie was the author of *David Copperfield*, *Oliver Twist*, and *The Old Curiosity Shop*, to name but a few.

This date saw the first Oxford and Cambridge boat race, in 1829. The clear winners were Oxford.

On this day in 1840, Edward Oxford, the servant in a pub, fired two shots at Queen Victoria and Prince Albert as they travelled up Constitution Hill, London, in an open carriage. Although he was only a few yards away from the carriage, Oxford missed them both. He was sent to a mental hospital, and was later released on condition that he went abroad.

On this day, 1809, Napoleon was excommunicated by the pope.

Today is a 'Dismal Day'. This day (and 23 others in the year) was thought to be unlucky in medieval times.

Some royal dates...
Prince Philip, the Duke of Edinburgh, was born today in Corfu, 1921.
King George I died today in 1727. Although King of England, George couldn't speak English.

Today was one of Henry VIII's wedding anniversaries. In fact, it was his first. On this day in 1509, he married Catherine of Aragon, the first of his six wives. The marriage had been arranged six years earlier, when Henry was 12.

On this day in 1903, the **King and Queen of Serbia** were murdered in their bedroom cupboard. But what were they doing in there in the first place?

On this day in 1667, the Dutch Admiral De Ruyter put the English navy to shame in a daring raid. He sailed up the Thames, destroyed several English ships and then towed away the pride of the English fleet, *The Royal Charles*. It was a great national humiliation.

King George II came to the throne on this day in 1727.

Jacques Cousteau, the French underwater explorer, was born this day in 1910. And **John Constable**, the English artist who painted *The Haywain* was born in 1776.

John Wayne, star of Hollywood westerns, finally lost his battle with the 'Big C' (as he called cancer), this day, 1979.

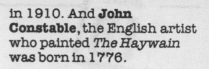

JUNE 12

On this day in 1701, Parliament passed the Act of Settlement. This established the House of Hanover (German) on the English throne, rather than the House of Stuart (Scottish).

Born today...
Anthony Eden, British Prime Minster for under two years in the 1950s. Born in 1897.
Charles Kingsley, author of *The Water Babies*, was born in Devon, 1819.

Sir Billy Butlin, founder of Butlin's Holiday Camps, died today in 1980...

Hi de Hi!

JUNE 13

On this day in 1842, Queen Victoria experienced her first train journey. She travelled from Slough to Paddington, where she was met by cheering crowds. Fortunately she didn't have to try a British Rail sandwich. She wrote...

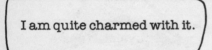

I am quite charmed with it.

13 June 1944: The first German V1 flying bomb exploded in London. The bomb, known as the 'Doodle Bug' was powered by a jet engine.

WB Yeats, the Irish poet and playwright, was born today in Dublin, 1865.
Alexander the Great, builder of the Greek Empire, died of malaria today in 323BC at the age of 33.

JUNE 14

On this day in 1940, Paris fell to Hitler as Nazi troops arrived in the city. The city was to remain under German occupation for four years.

On 14 June 1777, America adopted the stars and stripes as its flag at the Continental Congress. At that time, there were only 13 stars on the flag, one for each state of the union. The original flag was stitched together by Betsy Ross and presented to George Washington. This day is known as Flag Day in the US.

On this day in 1982, the Falkland Islands were rewon from Argentina by British troops. Shortly after the Argentinians in Stanley raised the white flag of surrender, the British raised the Union Jack.

The Vatican abolished the *Index of Forbidden Books* on this day, 1966. The *Index* listed books which Catholics were forbidden to read, and had been running since the days of the Inquisition in the 16th century.

Today's birthdays...
Mike Yarwood, the mimic, was born today in 1941.
Boy George was born today in 1961.
Harriet Beecher Stowe, the author of *Uncle Tom's Cabin*, born in 1811.

Che Guevara, Bolivian revolutionary, born 1928. His mum called him Ernesto.

JUNE
15

On this day in 1919, the first ever non-stop flight across the Atlantic was made by John Alcock and Arthur Brown. Their flight, from Newfoundland to a slightly undignified landing in an Irish bog lasted 16hrs 12mins, covering 1,900 miles.

On 15 June 1215, King John was forced by his barons to sign the Magna Carta ('Big Charter') at Runnymede, near Windsor. The charter limited the King's royal powers.

The first blood transfusion was carried out on a human being today in 1667. The French physician Jean-Baptiste Denys used lamb's blood on a 15-year-old boy, and it didn't seem to do him any harm...

A total eclipse of the Sun was witnessed in England today in the year 885.

On this day in 1752, Benjamin Franklin, the US scientist, flew a kite during a thunderstorm. The kite was flown on a metal wire, and Franklin was attempting to show the power of electricity. He was lucky to escape with his life...

JUNE 16

On this day in 1963, the first woman was blasted into space aboard the Russian *Vostok 6*. Valentina Tereshkova, a 26-year-old parachute jumper, spent the next three days in space, orbiting the Earth 48 times before returning.

On this day in 1961, the world-famous Russian ballet dancer, Rudolf Nureyev, defected to the West at Paris's Le Bourget airport. He ran towards French police shouting 'Protect me! Protect me!'

Today is a 'Dismal Day'. This day (and 23 others in the year) was thought to be unlucky in medieval times.

Mixed bathing was allowed for the first time in London's Serpentine, today in 1930.

Stan Laurel (of Laurel and Hardy fame) was born today in Lancashire, 1890. His real name was Arthur Stanley Jefferson. He sailed for America when he was 20.

JUNE 17

On this day in 1939, the last public execution by guillotine in France took place at Versailles. A large crowd got up early to see the murderer **Eugene Weidmann's** head roll at 4.50am.

The last German air raid on London in World War 1 took place today in 1918.

The Great Eastern, built as the largest ship in the world by Isambard Kingdom Brunel, started her maiden voyage across the Atlantic today in 1860. The passengers were not delighted to be on board. Despite the ship's luxuries, she rolled horribly and made everyone seasick.

On this day in 1944, Iceland was proclaimed an independent republic. It had belonged to Denmark since 1380.

Today sees two famous births...
King Edward I, who established English rule in Wales (and had a go at doing the same thing to the Scots). Born 1239.
John Wesley, the founder of Methodism who set a trend for open-air preaching. Born in Epworth, Lincolnshire, 1703.

JUNE 18

Today marks the Battle of Waterloo, in which Napoleon was finally defeated, 1815. The Duke of Wellington and the German General von Blücher fought against the French army at Waterloo in Belgium. Over 4,000 British and German troops died, and around 30,000 French were killed. Napoleon tried to raise another army, failed, and abdicated.

Waterloo Bridge, spanning the Thames in London, was opened this day in 1817.

A public beheading took place in Riyadh, Saudi Arabia, on this day in 1975. **Prince Museid** was executed for assassinating King Faisal.

Amelia Earhart became the first woman to fly the Atlantic on this day in 1928. She flew from Newfoundland to land her seaplane near Llanelli in South Wales.

Paul McCartney was born in Liverpool today in 1942.

Roald Amundsen, the first man to the South Pole, died when his aircraft crashed in the Arctic Ocean, today in 1928.

On this day in the year 325, the church Council of Nicaea first met. The council condemned the heretics of the time, agreed on the Christian doctrine of the trinity, produced the Nicene Creed (still recited in churches) and fixed the date for Easter in the Western Church. It was quite a busy time...

King James I was born on this day in 1566 in Edinburgh Castle. James had an obsessive love of lions, and kept them in the moat of the Tower of London. He was also paranoid about being assassinated, and always wore a padded waistcoat.

Today in 1917, the British royal family adopted the name of Windsor, and renounced their German titles. It wasn't a popular time to be German in Britain. World War 1 was still raging.

Today's births...
Salman Rushdie, famous for his novels and the death threat he received from the Ayatollah Khomenei. Born in India, 1947.

Blaise Pascal, the French mathematician and philosopher. Born in 1623.
Mrs Wallis Simpson (the woman King Edward VIII gave up his throne to marry). Born in Pennsylvania, 1896.
CH Spurgeon, the famous Victorian preacher. Born in 1834.

Julius and Ethel Rosenberg went to the electric chair in New York State on this day in 1953 for spying in the US. They were the first married couple to be executed in America.

JUNE 20

In the early hours of this morning in 1837, an 18-year old girl, Victoria, was woken to be told that she had become Queen of Great Britain. She was to rule for the rest of the nineteenth century.

On this day in 1963, the USSR and the US agreed to establish a hot line between the White House and the Kremlin. The line is permanently open, which must add up to a massive phone bill...

On the night of 20 June 1756, 146 British prisoners were crammed into a small cell in Calcutta. In the morning, 43 of the prisoners were found to have died. This atrocity (probably caused by lack of thought) became known as 'the black hole of Calcutta'.

JUNE 21

Today is the Summer Solstice, the longest day of the year. In Leap Years, the solstice falls on 22 June.

Prince William was born today in 1982. He is second in line to the throne after Charles, the Prince of Wales.

On this day in 1675, the first stone of the new St Paul's Cathedral in London was laid. The old cathedral had been burnt to the ground during the fire of London in September 1666. Sir Christopher Wren had designed the new cathedral.

Today in 1919 German seamen scuttled the German fleet, which had been captured by the British at the end of World War 1 and held at Scapa Flow in the Orkneys. Almost all of the 70 ships, valued at £50 million, went to the bottom.

JUNE 22

On this day in 1907, the Northern Line was opened on London's Underground.

King Richard II came to the English throne on this day in 1377. He was just 10 years old.

Today in 1911, King George V was crowned in Westminster Abbey. He then spent all afternoon answering letters and telegrams.

Born today...
Meryl Streep, the film actress who starred in *Kramer vs Kramer* and *The French Lieutenant's Woman*. She was born in 1949.
George Vancouver, explorer of the Pacific who gave his name to the Canadian city of Vancouver. Born in King's Lynn, Norfolk, 1758.
Billy Wilder, the film director of *Some Like It Hot*. Born in Vienna, 1906.

JUNE 23

Today is Midsummer's Eve, tomorrow being Midsummer's Day. In pagan times, chains of bonfires were lit around the country on 23 June. This was done to celebrate the power of the sun, which began to lose its power as the days grew shorter.

St Alban was beheaded on this day in AD286, during the persecution of Christians under the Roman Emperor, Diocletian. The place of his execution is now called St Albans.

On this day in 1985, an Air India Jumbo Jet exploded and crashed into the Atlantic 120 miles west of Ireland. The disaster was the work of a terrorist bomb.

Born on this day...
Joséphine, Empress and wife to Napoleon, born in 1763.
Charles Darwin, controversial evolutionist, born in 1809.
King Edward VIII, the king who abdicated for the woman he loved, born in 1894.

Henry Hudson, the English explorer, died soon after this day in 1611. America's River Hudson and Canada's Hudson's Bay are named after him. His crew mutinied in 1611 and they cast him adrift with eight other men. He was never seen again.

The Reign of Terror began in France on this day in 1793.

JUNE 24

Today is Midsummer's Day. Druids still gather at Stonehenge, after a sleepless night waiting for the sun to rise so they can start their services.

Today in 1902, King Edward VII had an operation for appendicitis. He was fortunate to survive - the operation was a very recent medical development.

On this day in 1830, Peter Bossey became the last person in England to suffer in the pillory. He was sentenced to six months in prison, one hour in the Old Bailey's pillory and seven years transportation to Australia.

Robert the Bruce, King of Scotland, defeated the English at the Battle of Bannockburn, this day in 1314.

This day was special for King Henry VIII. It was the day of his coronation, in 1509.

John of Gaunt, the Duke of Lancaster, was born this day in 1340.

Died on this day...
The Roman Emperor **Vespasian**, in Rome, AD79. The comedian **Tony Hancock** committed suicide in his hotel room in Sydney on this day in 1968.

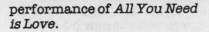

25 June 1876: US troops under the command of General George Custer were massacred by Sioux indians at the battle of the Little Big Horn (the name of a river), Montana. This event is known to history as 'Custer's Last Stand'.

The Korean War began today in 1950 when Communist North Korea invaded South Korea.

On this day in 1967, the first worldwide TV programme was seen by live satellite link in 26 countries by an estimated 400 million viewers. The programme, *Our World,* concluded with the Beatles' live performance of *All You Need is Love.*

Pope Innocent III was made pope on this day in 1243. Innocent was the first pope to give cardinals red hats.

Today's birthday personages...
Hermann Julius Oberth, the German rocket designer in charge of the V2 flying bombs that plagued London at the end of World War 2. Born in 1894.
George Orwell (his mum called him Eric Blair), the novelist who wrote *1984, Animal Farm* and numerous other books. Born in India, 1903.

On this day in 1963, President John F Kennedy visited Berlin, which was under a state of siege by Communist East Germany. To boost their morale he told the crowds: 'I am a

Berliner.' Unfortunately, 'berliner' is also German for a small doughnut...

On this day in 1948, the Columbia company officially unveiled their new 33.3rpm LP to the US press.

On 26 June 1483, Richard III seized the throne of England from his 12-year-old nephew Edward V, whom he was meant to protect. Edward was sent for a nice little holiday in the Tower of London, from which he and his younger brother never returned.

Three births today...
Laurie Lee, author of *Cider with Rosie,* born in Gloucestershire, 1914.
Lord William Kelvin, the physicist who invented his own scale of temperature, born in 1824.

Wilhelm Messerschmitt, the German aircraft engineer, was born in Frankfurt, 1898.

On this day in 1541, **Pizarro**, the Spanish conquistador who ruthlessly wiped out the Incas, was assassinated by Spanish conspirators in Lima, Peru.

JUNE 27

On this day in 1900, London Underground's Central Line was opened, connecting Shepherd's Bush to Bank. It was then called 'The Central London Electric Railway'.

Today in 1844, **Joseph Smith,** founder of the Church of Jesus Christ of Latter Day Saints (i.e. the Mormons),

was shot dead by rioters in Illinois. The Mormons weren't too popular in those days.

Born today: **Helen Keller,** who became both blind and deaf after an illness when she was 19 months old. Helen eventually learned how to speak and published her famous book, *The Story of My Life.* She was born in Alabama in 1880.

JUNE 28

28 June 1914: As Archduke Ferdinand (heir to the throne of Austria and Hungary) and his wife drove in an open car through Sarajevo, they were killed by two assassin's bullets. Earlier, a bomb had been lobbed into their car, but the Archduke had thrown it back out. The assassination sparked off World War 1.

Queen Victoria was crowned today in 1838. She was the first British monarch not to be anointed with the coronation oil on her chest. She was merely anointed on her head.

On this day in 1491, King Henry VII's wife gave birth to their third child: **Henry VIII**. His older brother Arthur was the heir to the throne, but he died leaving the way clear for young Harry.

By coincidence, the film *The King and I* (starring Yul Brunner) was released in the US today in 1956.

Today in 1905, mutiny broke out on the Russian battleship *Potemkin*, in the Black Sea. The crew rebelled after a sailor had been shot dead for complaining about the food.

Westminster Cathedral (the Roman Catholic place down the road from Westminster Abbey) was consecrated on this day in 1910.

JUNE 29

On this day in 1871, an act of Parliament made trade unions legal in Britain for the first time. Before 1871, people had been transported to Australia for belonging to a union.

The *Automobile Association* was formed today in 1905. One of their aims was to stop drivers from being arrested for breaking the 20mph speed limit.

I do hope we don't get stopped again for speeding...

The *Daily Telegraph* was founded on this day in 1855, as a 2d paper. Its price was later reduced to 1d. The Telegraph, now firmly Tory, started life as a Liberal newspaper.

JUNE
30

30 June 1908: At 7.17am, a massive fireball laid waste to a vast area of forest in northern Siberia. A farmer 60 kilometres away was knocked over and reported...

There appeared a great flash of light. There was so much heat that my shirt almost burned off my back. I saw a huge fireball that covered an enormous part of the sky...

Scientists now believe that the explosion was caused by a comet colliding with the Earth. But others think it

might have been a black hole, or a nuclear accident on board a UFO.

Alfred Hitchcock's *Psycho* (with its famous murder in the shower) opened today in 1960.

Charles Blondin made his first crossing on a high wire directly above Niagara Falls, on this day in 1859. Over the next few weeks, Blondin gave regular repeats of his stunt, but with added twists. He crossed the rope blindfold, carrying a man on his back, wheeling someone in a wheelbarrow, and even using stilts.

Today in 1841 the first railway link was opened between London and Bristol. The journey time was four hours, beating the stagecoach journey by 20 hours.

On this day in 1892, a shower of frogs fell on Birmingham, according to the locals. They were said to be almost white in colour. It happened around pub closing time...

30 June 1934 was the 'Night of the Long Knives' in Germany. Hitler's Nazis killed their political enemies, especially those who had been critical of Hitler's leadership.

Three Soviet cosmonauts on board a *Soyuz* space capsule were killed on this day in 1971, as their craft re-entered the Earth's atmosphere. They were found dead in their capsule after what had seemed to be a normal landing.

Died today...
Montezuma II, the last Aztec Emperor, was murdered at Tenochtitlán (now called Mexico City) by the Spaniards in 1520.
Johann Strauss, composer of the *Blue Danube* and other famous waltzes. He died in Vienna, 1899.

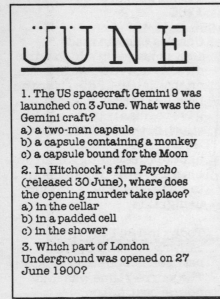

JÜNE

1. The US spacecraft Gemini 9 was launched on 3 June. What was the Gemini craft?
a) a two-man capsule
b) a capsule containing a monkey
c) a capsule bound for the Moon

2. In Hitchcock's film *Psycho* (released 30 June), where does the opening murder take place?
a) in the cellar
b) in a padded cell
c) in the shower

3. Which part of London Underground was opened on 27 June 1900?
a) the Central Line
b) the Jubilee Line
c) the Victoria Line

4. What was one of John Wayne's film catch phrases (he died 11 June)?
a) 'You ain't seen nothin' yet!'
b) 'The hell I will!'
c) 'I'm in charge!'

5. Who defeated the English on 18 June 1429?
a) William the Conqueror
b) Joan of Arc
c) Alexander the Great

Answers on page 272

JULY

Name

July was named *Quintilis* in the original Roman calendar. *Quintilis* comes from the Latin word for 'five' (we use it in 'quins' and 'quintet'). The month was called this because it was the fifth month in the Roman calendar, which was organized according to the phases of the moon.

In 44BC, Julius Caesar reorganized the calendar to follow the movements of the Sun and this became the seventh month. It was renamed *Julius* in his honour.

Red Letter Days

• 3 July marks the beginning of the 'Dog Days'
• 4 July is Independence Day in the United States
• 14 July is Bastille Day in France
• 15 July is St Swithin's Day
• 21 July is the anniversary of the first Moon landing in 1969

JULY 1

On this day in 1916, the first Battle of the Somme began during World War 1. This was the bloodiest battle in modern times. Over 1 million died. The battle came to an end four months later, on 8 November.

From this day in 1842, no British child under 16 could be apprenticed as a chimney sweep.

The world's longest-recorded sermon came to an end on this day in 1983. The Revd Ronald Gallagher finished his 120-hour epic at the Baptist Temple, Appomattox, USA. It is not known how many of his congregation were still awake.

On the royal front, today is **Princess Diana's** birthday, born in 1961. Prince Charles was invested as Prince of Wales at Caernarfon Castle, exactly eight years later, on this day in 1969. And today in 1872, Queen Victoria unveiled the Albert Memorial (in memory of her late husband) in London.

Died on this day...
Charles Goodyear, the inventor of vulcanized rubber, used in car tyres. He died in 1860.
Martin Luther, the monk who started the Protestant Reformation. Died in Germany, 1546.

JULY 2

On this day in 1900, the first Zeppelin airship left the ground for the skies. Count Ferdinand von Zeppelin, the ship's designer, took off from a field just outside Berlin. Zeppelins were used in World War 1 in the first-ever aerial bombardment of London.

On 2 July 1865, William Booth, a Methodist minister, conducted a religious service in a tent in London's East End. Out of this service, the Salvation Army was born, now alive and kicking in 86 countries around the world.

A heatwave in New York on this day in 1901 killed 400

New Yorkers. Temperatures soared to 110°F.

Today's birthdays...
Dr David Owen, SDP politician. Born in 1938.
Thomas Cranmer, Henry VIII's Archbishop of Canterbury. Born in 1489.

Today in 1644 saw the Battle of Marston Moor, a decisive battle of the English Civil War.

On this day, the world said goodbye to...
Nostradamus, the astrologer who predicted the future in his book *Centuries*. He died in France, 1566.
Ernest Hemingway, the novelist who wrote *For Whom the Bell Tolls*. It tolled for him today in 1961 after he committed suicide.

JULY 3

July 3rd marks the beginning of the 'Dog Days' for people living north of the equator. The Dog Days last until 15 August, and get their name from the rising of Sirius, the Dog Star. From Roman times, the rising and setting of Sirius was thought to cause summer's excessive heat and a host of calamities.

On this day in 1938, the steam engine *Mallard* set a new world record for steam engines. Roaring down the line from Newcastle to London, Mallard reached 126mph - a record still to be broken.

In the American Civil War between north and south, the Battle of Gettysburg ended on this day in 1863. The northern (anti-slavery) states won the battle, which proved to be a turning-point in the war.

On 3 July 1928, the first colour TV transmission was made by John Logie Baird.

Today marks **Tom Cruise's** birthday. Born in 1962.

JULY 4

4 July 1776 is famous in history. On this date, the United States issued its Declaration of Independence, opting out of British rule. Thomas Jefferson wrote the famous words, helped by Benjamin Franklin...

We hold these truths to be self-evident, that all men are created equal, that they are endowed by their Creator with certain unalienable Rights, that among these are Life, Liberty and the pursuit of Happiness.

On 4 July 1829, the first omnibus service in London was started by a Mr Shillibeer. The service ran between Paddington and the Bank of England.

On this day in 1976, Israeli commandos flew from Israel to Uganda, and in a pitched battle with Palestinian terrorists released over 100 Jewish hostages. The hostages had been hijacked and flown to Uganda's capital, Entebbe, and a deadline had been set for killing them.

The Statue of Liberty was presented to the United States by France today in 1883.

Born today...
Thomas Barnardo, founder of homes for homeless children. Born in Dublin, 1845.
Louis Armstrong, jazz trumpeter and singer, born in 1900.

JULY 5

Today is a day of firsts...

On this day in 1980, Bjorn Borg won the Wimbledon men's title for the fifth time in a row - the first man ever to do so. And on the same date in 1987, Martina Navratilova won the Wimbledon women's title for the sixth time in a row - another first ever!

The first BBC television news

broadcast was aired today in 1954.

Today also marked the first day of the new National Health Service, in 1948. From this date, everyone in Britain could receive free medical care.

The world's first travel agency, Thomas Cook, was founded on this day in 1841. It started business by booking the world's first excursion train, from Leicester to Loughborough.

JULY 6

On this day in 1483, Richard III was crowned King of England. He and the queen walked barefoot to their coronation in Westminster Abbey, which was the most sumptuous that century. His reign lasted just over two years.

Today in 1809, Pope Pius VII was taken prisoner by the French after he had dared to excommunicate Napoleon. Pius was held in captivity until he was allowed to return to Rome, five years later.

The Republican Party was formed in the United States on this day in 1854. Famous republicans have included Abraham Lincoln, Richard Nixon and Ronald Reagan.

Today's birthdays...
Sylvester Stallone, the film actor who starred in *Rocky* and *Rambo*. Born in 1946.
Bill Haley, 'the father of rock'n'roll', born in 1925. Bill Haley and the Comets electrified the early 1950s with *Rock Around the Clock*.

Martyred on this day...
John Huss, the church reformer in Prague who was burnt at the stake for criticizing the church.
Thomas More, beheaded in 1535 for refusing to acknowledge Henry VIII as head of the English church. As he put his head on the block. he pushed his beard aside, saying...

This hath not offended the king.

JULY 7

On this day in 1982, Queen Elizabeth II woke to find Mr Michael Fagan sitting on her bed in Buckingham Palace, swigging a bottle of wine that he had lifted from the royal wine cellar. She chatted to him for a while, and then summoned help when he asked for a cigarette.

Today in 1898, the island republic of Hawaii gave itself to the United States. Sixty years later, Hawaii was made a US state.

Born on this day...
James Cagney, film actor, born in New York City, 1904.
Ringo Starr, drummer for the Beatles, he sang in *I Get by with a Little Help from My Friends*. Born in Liverpool, 1940.

Died on this day...
King Edward I, fighting the Scots, 1307.
Arthur Conan Doyle, the creator of Sherlock Holmes, 1930.

JULY 8

The explorer Vasco da Gama left the port of Lisbon on this day in 1497. His voyage was to take him around the tip of South Africa to India. He was the first European to make this journey, and by doing it he opened up a new (and highly profitable) trade route.

On this day in 1901 a new speed limit was established for motor cars in France. Cars could now tear through French towns at the heady speed of 10kph (6mph).

Today saw a number of deaths...
Percy Shelley, the romantic poet, drowned during a storm while sailing off the coast of Italy in 1822.
Sir Harry Oakes, the gold-prospector who made millions, was murdered today in 1943.
Peter the Hermit, who preached the first crusade against Islam into existence, died today in 1108.

JULY 9

On this night in 1984, the 700-year-old roof of York Minster was set ablaze by a bolt of lightning. The bolt fell just a week after the controversial Bishop of Durham was consecrated inside the building. Many believed it was a sign of divine impatience...

A cat interrupted a House of Commons debate today in 1874.

The newly-completed Tower Bridge was opened to the public for the first time on this day in 1894.

Lady Jane Grey was proclaimed Queen of England on this day in 1553. She ruled for just 11 days.

Henry VIII divorced his fourth wife, Anne of Cleves, on 9 July 1540. For good looks, he rated her 0.

Simon Marks (of Marks and Spencer) was born today in 1888.

JULY 10

Today in 1962, *Telstar 1* was launched. It was the first-ever telecommunications satellite and made it possible for live television pictures to be seen across the Atlantic.

On 10 July 1588, the Spanish Armada sailed from the Spanish port of Corunna, destination, England. The plan was for the Armada to ferry Spanish troops across the Channel from Belgium to invade England.

Today in 1923, Benito Mussolini, fascist dictator of Italy, outlawed all political parties other than his own. A few days later, he also banned gambling in Italy.

Who died today?
The Roman Emperor **Hadrian**, who built Hadrian's Wall, dividing England from Scotland. He died in Italy, AD138.
Louis Daguerre, French inventor of an early form of photography, known as the daguerreotype. He died in 1851.

JULY 11

Today marks one of the great milestones in human history. On 11 July 1950, Andy Pandy (together with Teddy and short-skirted Looby Loo) was first broadcast on television.

The following people also made their mark on this day...
Robert the Bruce, King of Scotland, was born today in 1274.
Theodore Maiman, inventor of the laser, was born in Los Angeles, today in 1927.
The Aga Khan, head of the Ismaili sect of Islam, died on this day, 1957.

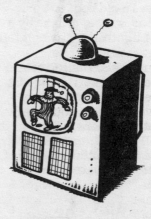

JULY 12

On this day in 1910, **Charles Rolls** (of Rolls-Royce) became the first Briton to die in a plane crash. He was flying his biplane in a competition at Eastbourne when the rudders broke and the plane hurtled to the ground.

Henry VIII married his sixth (and final) wife, Catherine Parr, at Hampton Court on this day in 1543. Catherine had been married twice before, and after Henry's death married again. She is England's most-married queen.

Today's birthday boys...
Julius Caesar, the Roman Emperor who invaded Britain. Julius was born in 100BC.
Josiah Wedgewood, the potter who created the famous blue-and-white china, born today in 1730.
George Eastman, the photographic pioneer who gave his name to Eastman-Kodak. Born in New York, 1854.

Taijde Khan (screen name, Yul Bruyner), who starred in *The Magnificent Seven* and many other films. Born in 1915.

JULY 13

13 July 1985: The Live Aid concert, called 'the biggest concert in history', was staged simultaneously in Wembley Stadium, England, and JFK Stadium, USA. Some of the greatest names in rock music sang to aid starving Africa. The concert was beamed live to 160 countries through satellite link-ups and reached an estimated television audience of 1 billion people.

On this day in 1837, Queen Victoria moved house. Her new address was: Buckingham Palace, London SW1. The old palace had been newly-renovated.

Today is a 'Dismal Day'. In medieval times this day was considered unlucky.

Today in 1955, 28-year-old **Ruth Ellis** was hanged at Holloway Prison for the murder of her ex-lover David Blakely. She shot him twice in the back for leaving her.

The judge told the jury that jealousy was no defence in English law. She was the last woman to hang in Britain.

On this day in 1977, New York was plunged into darkness due to a total power failure. The black-out was welcomed by criminals, who made the most of it with looting and vandalism. Mayor Beame declared a state of emergency.

JULY 14

This day is celebrated as Bastille Day in France. On it, the French remember the storming of the Bastille in 1789, which signalled the start of the French Revolution. The Bastille was a formidable medieval castle, used as a prison in Paris. Only seven prisoners were found inside, but the Bastille was demolished and its governor killed.

On this day in 1868, dynamite was first tested and approved in Sweden. The inventor of dynamite was Alfred Nobel, who used the millions he made from his explosives to set up the Nobel Peace Prize, and the other Nobel prizes!

Some famous births...
Gerald Ford, US President after Nixon resigned, was born today in 1913.
Emmeline Pankhurst was also born on this day, 1858. Emmeline was a famous campaigner for women's rights.
Woody Guthrie, the American folk singer, was born in Oklahoma today, 1912.
Sue Lawley, newsreader, television presenter and chat-show host. She was born in 1946.

JULY 15

Today is St Swithin's Day. Legend has it that the weather on this day determines the weather for the next 40 days. St Swithin was a 9th-century Bishop of Winchester. When it was proposed to move his remains to the cathedral, 40 days of foul weather followed. This was taken as a none-too-gentle hint to leave Swithin alone!

On this day in 1099, the Crusaders (an army of European troops) seized Jerusalem, which had been under Muslim rule for 450 years. Their control of Jerusalem was to last only 88 years, when it was recaptured by the Muslims.

On 15 July 1685, **James Scott**, the Duke of

Monmouth, was executed for treason on Tower Hill, London. The illegitimate son of King Charles II, Monmouth had tried to claim the crown from King James II, but his rebellion failed miserably. His last words...

> Prithee, let me feel the axe. I fear it is not sharp enough. Do not hack me as you did my Lord Russell.

At 1.20am on 15 July 1965, the US space probe *Mariner IV* began to take close-up pictures of Mars as it swept within a few thousand miles of the planet. The pictures it sent were the first close-ups of Mars ever seen.

The Dutch painter, **Rembrandt**, was born today in 1606.

JULY 16

The Muslim era began on this day in the year 622 when Muhammad fled from the city of Medina in Saudi Arabia because of persecution. This event is known to Muslims as the *Hegira*.

Apollo XI, the first American mission to land on the moon, was launched at 9.32am, today in 1969.

The world's first atomic explosion took place on this day in 1945, at Los Alamos, New Mexico. Just 17 days later, the bomb was dropped on Hiroshima. Robert Oppenheimer, the physicist in charge of the test recalled some words from Hindu scripture as he saw the explosion:

> I am become death, the destroyer of worlds.

Tsar Nicholas II of Russia and his family were murdered in cold blood on this day in 1918. They were shot and bayoneted by Bolsheviks (who had led the Russian Revolution) in a cellar in Ekaterinberg.

JULY 17

On this day in 1975, two space craft met and docked in Earth orbit. It was the first-ever meeting of a US *Apollo* and a Russian *Soyuz*. Over the next three days, the Russians and Americans visited each other, shared meals and jokes together and appeared on television.

The Queen opened the Humber Bridge on this day in 1981. The bridge was (and remains) the longest cable suspension bridge in the world, stretching over 1.3 miles.

Today in 1819 the United States bought the territory of Florida from Spain.

Some famous birthdays...
Isaac Watts, the hymnwriter, was born in 1674. He wrote

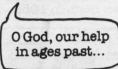

O God, our help in ages past...

Lloyd George, the Liberal Prime Minister, was born today in 1863.
James Cagney, Hollywood actor, was born in 1899. One of his most famous lines...

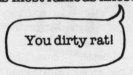

You dirty rat!

JULY 18

On this day in 1870, a church council in Rome declared that the pope was infallible when speaking on matters of great importance.

On 18 July 1987, Oxford University refused for the second time to award Mrs Thatcher an honorary degree. They refused as a protest at the conservative policy of educational cutbacks.

Disneyland opened just outside Los Angeles, today in 1955. The whole thing had cost $17 million to build.

Born on this day...
WG Grace, the great

Victorian cricketer who put cricket on the map, 1848. **Richard Branson**, the entrepreneurial business- man whose career spans record stores, publishing, and ballooning across the Atlantic. Born in 1950.

Vidkun Quisling, the Nazi collaborator in Norway who was made puppet ruler of the country during the war. Born in 1887. **John Glenn**, the famous American astronaut. Born in Ohio, 1921.

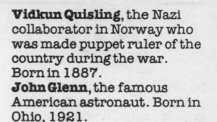

JULY
19

The great fire of ancient Rome began on this day in AD64. Rome burned for six days and seven nights. Gangs of men who said they were acting 'under orders' prevented people from putting the fires out. The Emperor Nero returned from a holiday to admire 'the beauty of the flames', put on a tragic robe and played the lyre as he watched. It has always been suspected that he ordered the fire for his own amusement, or as an excuse to rebuild and expand his palace.

The first solo rowing of the Atlantic was completed on this day in 1969. An exhausted but happy John Fairfax reached Fort Lauderdale in Florida, after a 180-day journey.

Mary, daughter of Henry VIII, became Queen of England today in 1553. She became known as 'Bloody Mary' because of her persecution of protestants.

Today in 1821, King George IV was crowned with great extravagance in Westminster Abbey. His wife, Queen Caroline (whom he loathed), tried to get into the cathedral at its different doors, but was refused entry each time as she didn't have a ticket.

JULY 20

Singles charts were published for the first time on this day in 1940 by Billboard magazine. The first No. 1 was *I'll Never Smile Again* by Tommy Dorsey.

The *Mary Rose,* Henry VIII's flagship, sank in the Solent today in 1545 with great loss of life. Henry watched from the shore as the ship rolled over because it was overloaded.

News from space...
A US *Viking* spacecraft soft-landed on Mars today in 1976, after an 11-month journey. It snapped the first close-up pictures of the surface of Mars. Meanwhile, on the Moon, *Apollo XI's* Lunar Module touched down on the Sea of Tranquility on this day in 1969. The two astronauts

inside were the first men ever to visit another body in space.

20 July 1944: A suitcase bomb exploded under a table a few feet away from Adolf Hitler. Three people were killed, but Hitler was virtually unharmed. A few hours later, his staff officer, **von Stauffenberg**, was executed for his part in the plot.

On 20 July 1588, news reached Plymouth that the Spanish Armada had been sighted from the Isles of Scilly, heading towards the English Channel. Sir Francis Drake was playing bowls when the news broke, but instead of dashing to his ship he is supposed to have said...

There is plenty of time to win this game, and to thrash the Spaniards too.

JULY 21

21 July 1969: At 2.56am (Greenwich time) the US astronaut Neil Armstrong

climbed down the ladder of his Lunar Module and walked out onto the surface of the moon. He was the first person ever to do so. He and Buzz Aldrin (who was still in the Lunar Module) were

250,000 miles from home. As Armstrong planted his foot on lunar soil, he said...

> That's one small step for a man, one giant leap for mankind.

They spent the rest of the day collecting rocks and taking photos of each other.

Today in 1873 saw the first Wild West train robbery at Adair, Iowa. The hold-up was carried out by the James-Younger gang.

Today's births...
Paul von Reuter, the founder of Reuter's news agency, Germany 1816.
Ernest Hemingway, the novelist who wrote *For Whom the Bell Tolls*, Illinois 1899.

Died today...
Albert Luthuli, the Zulu chief who urged non-violence in South Africa. He died in 1967.
Robert Burns, Scottish national poet. Died in 1796.

JULY
22

On this day in 1878, an act was passed in Parliament to prevent medically untrained people from calling themselves 'dentists'. It's bad enough being drilled by trained dentists...

The first around-the-world solo plane journey was completed today in 1933. Wiley Post's flight was completed in just under eight days.

Today is a 'Dismal Day'. In medieval times this day (along with 23 other days throughout the year) was considered unlucky.

Revd William Archibald Spooner was born on 22 July 1844. Spooner is remembered as the creator of spoonerisms (where the first letters of two words are switched) which often reduced his listeners to tears of laughter. His most famous spoonerism was...

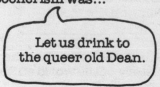

> Let us drink to the queer old Dean.

JULY 23

On this day in 1965, the Beatles single *Help!* was released in Britain.

The Ford Motor Company sold its first production car today in 1903. The car was the two-cylinder Model A Ford.

On 23 July 1970, two CS Gas cannisters were lobbed into the chamber of the House of Commons. The gas was being used against street rioters in Northern Ireland.

Today's birthday personages...
Emperor Haile Selassie was born today in 1892. He ruled Ethiopia from 1916 to 1974. Haile Selassie is at the heart of Rastafarianism.
Isaac Singer, the inventor in the US of the Singer sewing machine. He was born in Torquay, Devon, in 1875.

JULY 24

On 24 July 1969, the *Apollo XI* astronauts returned safely to Earth. After splashing down in the Pacific, President Nixon greeted them by calling the landing on the Moon:

The greatest week in the history of the world since the Creation.

On this day in 1704, Admiral Sir George Rooke took Gibraltar from Spain. Gibraltar has remained in British hands ever since, despite Spanish protests.

Today in 1851 saw the abolition of what must be Britain's most crazy tax ever - the Window Tax. The more windows you had, the more tax you paid, which is why many people had their windows bricked up!

Captain Matthew Webb, the

first man to swim the English Channel, drowned while attempting to swim across the whirlpool rapids at Niagara Falls, this day in 1883.

Some births and deaths...
Peter Sellers, the comedian who gave us the Goons and Inspector Clouseau of the Pink Panther films, died today in 1980.
Simón Bolívar, who liberated Bolivia from Spain and gave the country his name, was born today in 1783.
Alexandre Dumas, the author of *The Three Musketeers* was born today in 1802.

JULY 25

Louis Blériot became the first person to fly across the English Channel today in 1909. His 43-minute flight from Calais to Dover won him the £1,000 prize offered by the *Daily Mail*.

Today also saw the first crossing of the Channel by a hovercraft, which took two hours.

A wave of highway shootings continued on the Los Angeles freeway system today in 1987. The driver of a Volkswagen caused offence by driving too slowly, and was shot dead by a man in a passing truck.

Thomas Edison showed off his latest invention at the Savoy Hotel, today in 1890. He had made the world's first talking dolls. The dolls were fitted with a hidden record player powered by clockwork, and could jabber up to 30 words.

Today saw two deaths...
Charles Macintosh, inventor of the plastic mac. Died 1843.
Samuel Taylor Coleridge, the poet who wrote *Kubla Khan* and *The Rime of the Ancient Mariner*. He died in 1834. Some of Coleridge's most famous lines (from *the Ancient Mariner*) are...

> Water, water, everywhere, Nor any drop to drink...

JULY 26

On this day in 1987, monkeys escaped from their transportation crates at Moscow International airport and started using the airport lifts. Not surprisingly, their action caused major disruption to passengers.

Close to midnight on 26 July 1978, the world's first test-tube baby, **Louise Brown**, was born. She weighed in at 5lbs 12ozs.

Today's other (non-test-tube) births...

Mick Jagger, lead singer with the Rolling Stones, famous for his on-stage strutting and pouting lips, was born in Dartford, Kent, 1944.

George Bernard Shaw, the Irish dramatist, was born in Dublin, 1856.

Eva Perón, popularly-loved wife of the Argentinian leader (and subject of the musical *Evita*) died on this day in 1952.

JULY 27

Britain and the North American continent were electrically connected on this day in 1866, when the first Atlantic cable was brought ashore at Newfoundland. The cable was laid on the sea bed by Brunel's *Great Eastern*, which started out life as a luxury liner.

Apart from that, there is only one birth to report.

Hilaire Belloc, known for his Cautionary Tales for children, was born this day in 1870. He once wrote...

When I am dead, I hope it may be said:
'His sins were scarlet, but his books were read.'

JULY 28

28 July 1588: Soon after midnight, ships loaded with tar and explosives were sent into the heart of the Spanish Armada, which was moored off the coast of Calais. The Spanish cut their anchors and fled before the burning mass of ships. As the fleet broke up, the Armada threat to England was over.

Henry VIII privately married his fifth wife, the gorgeous, pouting Catherine Howard, on this day in 1540. Catherine, who was Henry's most attractive wife, was declared queen 11 days later. She was executed for adultery after 17 months of marriage.

Antonio Vivaldi, the composer of *The Four Seasons*, died today in Vienna, 1741.
Johann Sebastian Bach, hailed as the greatest classical composer, died in Liepzig today in 1750.

JULY 29

On this day in 1981, amid great rejoicing, Prince Charles married Lady Diana Spencer at St Paul's Cathedral, London.

On 29 July 1968, Pope Paul VI issued his latest encyclical, with the snappy title *Humanae Vitae* ('On Human Life'). The encyclical forbad the birth-control pill to Catholics. There was worldwide protest among catholics.

The world's first Boy Scouts pitched their tents and straightened their woggles on Brownsea Island, Poole, today in 1907. They were probably singing: *Ging-gang goolie-goolie-goolie-goolie wash gang ging-gang goo, ging-gang goo...* From this camp, the Boy Scout movement grew.

At 1am, **Vincent Van Gogh**, the Dutch painter, died after shooting himself two days earlier in a field. He died in his brother's arms.

JULY 30

On 30 July 1966, the final of the World Cup was played in Wembley Stadium. In an edge-of-the-seat match, England, captained by Bobby Moore, beat Germany 4-2 in extra time. It was England's first World Cup win.

On this day in 1963, Kim Philby, the British intelligence officer who spied for the Russians, was granted refuge in the USSR. Philby was known as 'the Third Man', as he was the third in a Soviet spy-ring. He later became a KGB general.

Captain Cook set sail on his first voyage of exploration in the *Endeavour* on this day in 1768. His mission was to observe the transit of Venus across the sun, something that could only be seen in the southern hemisphere. He circumnavigated the world and returned home on 12 June 1771.

Happy birthdays to...
Daley Thompson, decathlon record-breaker, born in 1958.
Henry Ford, world's first mass-produced car manufacturer, born in Michigan, 1863.
Emily Brontë, the author of the novel *Wuthering Heights*, born in Yorkshire, 1818.
Kate Bush, pop singer born in 1958.

JULY 31

Dr Crippen, who murdered his wife with poison, was arrested at sea on this day in 1910, as he and his mistress, Ethel Le Neve, were making their escape to Canada. Crippen had shaved his moustache and Neve was dressed as his son, but the ship's captain saw them holding hands on deck and matched them to a newspaper description. He used his radio to alert Scotland Yard - and the arrest became the first achieved by radio.

On this day in 1971, two astronauts went for a drive on the Moon. David Scott and Jim Irwin drove the moon buggy (officially called the *Lunar Roving Vehicle*) over the bumpy surface steering only with the back wheels. The front steering had jammed.

The singer **Jim Reeves** died in a US plane crash today in 1964. However, Jim's career was relatively unaffected. The singer had recorded loads of songs that hadn't yet been released, so new Jim Reeves numbers were to hit the charts for many years to come!

K2, the world's second highest mountain (in north India), was first climbed on this day in 1954 by an Italian climbing team.

Christopher Columbus discovered Trinidad, today in 1498.

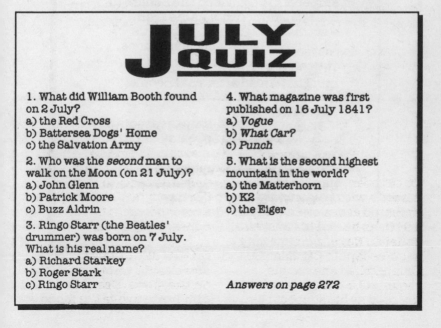

JULY QUIZ

1. What did William Booth found on 2 July?
a) the Red Cross
b) Battersea Dogs' Home
c) the Salvation Army

2. Who was the *second* man to walk on the Moon (on 21 July)?
a) John Glenn
b) Patrick Moore
c) Buzz Aldrin

3. Ringo Starr (the Beatles' drummer) was born on 7 July. What is his real name?
a) Richard Starkey
b) Roger Stark
c) Ringo Starr

4. What magazine was first published on 16 July 1841?
a) *Vogue*
b) *What Car?*
c) *Punch*

5. What is the second highest mountain in the world?
a) the Matterhorn
b) K2
c) the Eiger

Answers on page 272

▼august◄

Name
In Roman times, August was known as *Sextilis* (meaning 'the sixth month'). After Julius Caesar added January and February to the Roman year, this became the eighth month, but they kept calling it Sextilis because the army still used the old system.

Then in 8BC, the Emperor Augustus (one of the greatest Roman emperors) persuaded the Senate to change the month's name from *Sextilis* to *Augustus*. And that's what it has been called ever since.

July and August are the only two months named after real people.

Red Letter Days
• 6 August is remembered by many people around the world as Hiroshima Day
• 15 August is VJ (Victory over Japan) Day, marking the event that ended World War 2 in 1945

AUG 1

1 August 1914: Germany declared war on Russia, and the opening shots of World War 1 were fired. By the end of the month, the Russians had suffered a colossal defeat as the Germans advanced into Russian territory.

Glen Miller and his band recorded *In the Mood* on this day in 1939.

Today is a 'Dismal Day' - believed in the middle ages to be unlucky.

On 1 August 1798, Lord Nelson fought one of his greatest sea battles. At the Battle of the Nile, he almost completely destroyed Napoleon's fleet.

Today in 1834 marked the abolition of slavery in the British Empire. 770,280 slaves were declared free.

On this day in 1732, the foundation stone was laid for the Bank of England, in London's Threadneedle Street.

Oxygen was discovered on this day in 1774 by Joseph Priestley. People had been breathing in the stuff for years without noticing it...

Queen Anne died on 1 August 1714. And in 1819 **Herman Melville**, the author of *Moby Dick*, was born.

AUG 2

On this day in 1100, **King William II** (son of William the Conqueror) was killed in a hunting accident in the New Forest. An arrow shot by Walter Tyrrel glanced off a tree and hit the king. A triangular stone still marks the spot where it happened.

Today in 1774, the first mail coach left London for Bristol. The journey took over 24 hours.

August 2nd is remembered more for deaths than births. Here they are...
Thomas Gainsborough, the artist famous for his portraits. He died in 1788.
Wild Bill Hickok, the marshal of Kansas City, who

gunned down many outlaws. Bill was shot in the back on this day in 1876.

Alexander Graham Bell, the inventor of the telephone,

died in 1922.

Louis Blériot, who made the first English Channel crossing in a plane. He died in 1936.

Christopher Columbus set sail on his first expedition to the New World on this day in 1492. They sailed from Palos in Andalusia, with three Spanish vessels, hoping to reach India and Asia - but they discovered America instead. They didn't see land again for two months.

On this day in 1858, John Speke became the first European to see Lake Victoria, the source of the River Nile.

Henry Hudson also discovered something on this day in 1610. His ship sailed into Hudson Bay in north-eastern Canada.

Calvin Coolidge, son of a shopkeeper, became the 30th US President today in 1923. Coolidge was known as a man of few words. He was once asked what a preacher

had said in his sermon on sin...

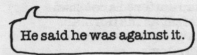

He said he was against it.

Born today...

Terry Wogan, broadcaster and chat-show host. Born in 1938.

Elisha Graves Otis, who developed the first safety elevator. Elisha was born in Vermont, USA, in 1811.

Stanley Baldwin, British Prime Minister in the 1920s and 30s. Born in 1876.

AUG 4

On this day in 1914, Britain declared war on Germany and entered World War 1. The war was to last for four years. On the same day, America declared that it was staying neutral.

The last set of stocks was taken down in London at St Clement Danes (in the Strand) today in 1826. The stocks were used to fasten the feet or arms of criminals, so that they could be pelted with rotten eggs and other objects.

Born today...
Percy Bysshe Shelley, the 19th-century romantic poet. Born in Sussex, 1792.
Elizabeth Bowes-Lyon (now known as the Queen Mother). As the wife of King George VI, she was crowned Queen Consort in 1937. Born today in 1900.

AUG 5

On this day in 1962, the actress **Marilyn Monroe** was discovered dead in her home. She was found holding the telephone receiver and with an empty bottle of tablets by her side. She spoke her final words to her housekeeper the night before...

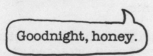

Goodnight, honey.

On 5 August 1939, the first transatlantic airmail service began.

Henry I became King today in 1100, after his father, William Rufus (meaning William Red-face) was accidentally killed in the New Forest.

Born on this day...
Neil Armstrong, the first man on the moon. Born in Ohio, 1930.
Sean Connery, the film actor who starred in the first James Bond movies. He was born on exactly the same day as Neil Armstrong, in 1930.

AUG 6

6 August 1945: At 8.16am, the world's first atom bomb was dropped on Hiroshima. The bomb, nicknamed 'Little Boy' was dropped from a US plane and had the power of 12,500 tons of TNT. Over 155,000 people died within a year as a direct result.

On this day in 1926, Gertrude Ederle, a 19-year old New Yorker, became the first woman to swim the English Channel. She also set another record, for the fastest crossing, by more than two hours.

The electric chair was used for the first time in the US on 6 August 1890. **William Kemmler** went to the chair in Auburn Prison, New York

State.

Today's births...
Alfred Lord Tennyson, the Victorian Poet Laureate, was born in 1810.
Robert Mitchum, Hollywood actor, was born in Connecticut, USA, in 1917.

Today's deaths...
Anne Hathaway, William Shakespeare's wife, died in 1623.
Ben Jonson, the famous playwright who started life as a brickie. Died today in 1637.

I still think it'd be better with armbands...

AUG 7

On this day in 1942, during World War 2, US marines landed at the Pacific island of Guadalcanal. This signalled the beginning of the

Japanese retreat in the Pacific.

Mata Hari, the dancer who passed military secrets to German spies during World War 1, was born today in the Netherlands, 1876.

164

8 August 1963: At 3.10am, 15 armed and masked men stopped the London mail train just outside Cheddington in Buckinghamshire. The train was loaded with used banknotes on their way to be destroyed. After breaking into the mail vans, the Great Train Robbers drove off with an estimated £2.5 million.

At 9pm on this day in 1974, President Richard Nixon appeared on US television to announce his resignation due to the Watergate scandal. He had been involved in illegal activities during his election campaign. Nixon was the only US President ever to resign.

I shall resign the presidency effective at noon tomorrow.

Today in 1767, Mt Vesuvius in Italy (which buried Pompeii in AD79) gave a fearsome series of eruptions.

The musical *Jesus Christ Superstar* opened at the Palace Theatre, London, on this day in 1972.

The stone of destiny, a lump of rock on which all Scotland's ancient kings had been crowned, was brought to England on this day in 1296. The stone had been kept at Scone, but it is still part of the Coronation Chair in Westminster Abbey. All of England's monarchs since Edward II have been crowned on it.

On 8 August 1588, Queen Elizabeth I gave a famous (but slightly sexist) speech to her troops at Tilbury, on the eve of the Spanish Armada triumph...

I know I have the body of a weak and feeble woman, but I have the heart and stomach of a king, and a king of England, too.

Today is a birthday for the actor **Dustin Hoffman**. Hoffman has starred in films such as *Tootsie*, *Kramer vs Kramer* and *Rain Man*. He was born today in 1937.

AUG 9

On 9 August 1945, the second atomic bomb, code-named 'Fat Boy' was dropped on the Japanese city of Nagasaki by the United States. Japan surrendered only five days later, bringing World War 2 to an end.

The Persians won the Battle of Thermopylae against the Spartans, who had fought to the death, on this day in 480BC.

Gerald Ford was sworn in as the 38th US President today in 1974. He took over from Richard Nixon, who had just resigned. The Chief Justice had to be flown from a holiday in Europe to administer the oath.

Thomas Telford, the builder of the Menai Suspension Bridge, was born today in 1757.
The Roman Emperor **Trajan** died on this day, AD117.

AUG 10

On this day in 1842, the Mines and Collieries Act was passed in Parliament. The new act, presented by the great reformer Lord Shaftesbury, prevented women and young children from working in the terrible conditions underground.

The Royal Greenwich Observatory was founded on this day in 1675. The Greenwich meridian (0° longitude) still passes through the observatory.

On 11 August 1877, the two moons that circle Mars were first seen by the US astronomer Asaph Hall. They were named Phobos and Deimos. Phobos (the larger moon) is only 17 miles wide and orbits Mars three times a day.

On this day in 1711, Queen Anne called the first race meeting at Ascot. Anne was very keen on horses, just like her uncle, Charles II.

Today in 1909 saw the first use of the SOS distress signal.

The new Waterloo Bridge was opened to traffic on this day in 1942.

Enid Blyton, the children's author and creator of the Famous Five, was born this day in 1897.

Today is known as 'the Glorious Twelfth' - the date when grouse-shooting officially begins.

The next total eclipse of the Sun visible in England will take place on this day in 1999.

On this day in 1908, the Model T Ford was first produced in Detroit. It was the first cheap motor car. It was nicknamed the 'Tin Lizzy', was the first car with a left-hand steering wheel, and, as Henry Ford boasted...

> You can have any colour you like, as long as it's black.

Died on this day...
George Stephenson, who built the *Rocket,* Britain's first steam locomotive. George died in Chesterfield today in 1848.
William Blake, the poet and artist, died today in 1827.
Ian Fleming, the creator of the James Bond books, died on this day in 1964.

AUG 13

On this day in 1942, the Walt Disney classic *Bambi* received its world premiere at Radio City Music Hall, New York.

On 13 August 1792, the French royal family was arrested and thrown into prison. The king, Louis XVI was deprived of his title in September and guillotined the following January.

Born on this day...
Fidel Castro, the President of Cuba. Fidel was born to wealthy parents today in 1927.
Alfred Hitchcock, film director and master of suspense. Alfred was born to a Leytonstone greengrocer on this day, 1899.
John Logie Baird, who pioneered the invention of television, was born in Scotland, 1888.

Died on this day...
HG Wells, the author of numerous books, including *The Time Machine* and *The Invisible Man* died today in 1946.
Florence Nightingale, pioneering nurse during the Crimean War, died this day, 1910.

AUG 14

On this day in 1945, the Japanese finally surrendered to the Allies, signalling the end of World War 2. The Japanese Emperor, Hirohito, agreed to the allied terms of surrender. The cost of World War 2 was greater than the cost of all the wars in history added together.

On this day in 1930, the Church of England cautiously said 'yes' to birth control.

Augustus Montague Toplady was born on this day in 1778. Augustus was the hymn writer who thought up *Rock of Ages* while sheltering

in a cracked rock during a
violent thunderstorm.

Two newspapermen died
today...
Alfred Harmsworth
(Viscount Northcliffe) who
founded the Daily Mail. He
died in London, 1922.
Randolph Hearst, US
newspaper magnate. He died
in California, 1951. Hearst
was the model for Orson
Welles' *Citizen Kane*.

Hold the
obituaries column!

AUG 15

Today is VJ Day (Victory
over Japan Day), when the
end of World War 2 was
celebrated in 1945 by the
Allies around the world.
Japan had fought on for two
months after Germany had
surrendered.

The Panama Canal,
connecting the Atlantic and
Pacific Oceans was opened on
this day in 1914.

On this day in 1877, the
human voice was first
recorded. Thomas Alva
Edison made the historic
recording on his invention,
the phonograph. He recited
Mary Had a Little Lamb, at

Menlo Park, USA, rotating a
cylinder covered with tin foil
operated by a hand crank.

Today's birthday persons...
Princess Anne, the second
child of Queen Elizabeth II,
was born in 1950.
Napoleon Bonaparte was
born today in Corsica, 1769.
TE Lawrence ('Lawrence of
Arabia'), who wrote *The
Seven Pillars of Wisdom*. He
was born in Wales, 1888.

Today's deaths...
Macbeth, the King of
Scotland who stars in
Shakespeare's play
Macbeth, died today in 1057.
René Magritte, the Belgian
surrealist painter with a
sense of humour, died in
1967.

16 August 1977: **Elvis Presley**, the King of Rock'n'Roll, was found dead in his mansion home, Graceland, in Memphis, Tennessee. Elvis was 42 years old and had died of a drug overdose.

On this day in 1965, the Beatles were paid a record $160,000 for a single concert appearance at New York's Shea Stadium. The screaming of the fans, infected with Beatlemania, was so loud that the group could have got away without playing a note.

On this day in 1819, crowds gathered in St Peter's Fields, Manchester, to listen to speakers calling for political reform in England. The gathering was illegal, and to break it up, soldiers charged into the crowd, guns firing. Eleven people were killed and 500 were wounded. The massacre became known as Peterloo.

Charlie Chaplin's film, *Gold Rush,* opened in the US today in 1925.

Today's birth and death...
Madonna Louise Veronica Ciccone, known to the world simply as Madonna, was born today in 1959.
Robert Bunsen, inventor of the bunsen burner, died this day in 1899.

AUG 17

On this day in 1987, **Rudolf Hess** died at Spandau Prison in West Berlin. He was said to have strangled himself with some electrical wire, but this claim was disputed by his relatives. Hess, deputy to Adolf Hitler from 1933-41, had been imprisoned during World War 2, and had served 41 years behind bars at Spandau.

This day saw a number of births...
Mae West, film star and sex symbol, was born today in 1892. Her most famous line was...

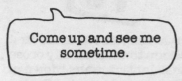

Come up and see me sometime.

William Carey, pioneering Baptist missionary to India, was born this day in 1761. **Davy Crockett**, wild west hero, was born in Tennessee, 1786.

Frederick the Great, one of the greatest soldiers of all time, died this day, 1786.

AUG 18

On this day in 1503, **Pope Alexander VI**, the infamous Borgia Pope, was suddenly taken ill at a meal and shortly afterwards died. It is suspected that he had intended to poison his host, a cardinal, but that the drinks were switched at the last moment. His illegitimate daughter, Lucrezia Borgia, took after her Dad as a poisoner.

Robert Redford, screen actor in films such as *Butch Cassidy and the Sundance Kid,* and director of films such as *Ordinary People,* was born today in 1937.

Genghis Khan, the Mongol emperor whose empire spanned the lands between the Yellow Sea and the Black Sea, died today in 1227.

AUG 19

On this day in 1978, the first balloon to successfully cross the Atlantic touched down in a French field west of Paris. The balloon, *Double Eagle II*, carried three pilots who had endured six miserable days aloft, pounded by the jet stream's sub-zero temperatures and by freezing rain.

19 August 1987: Michael Ryan, armed with a hunting rifle and a sub-machine-gun, shot 14 people dead, including his mother, and wounded 15 others as he walked through his home town of Hungerford. The Hungerford Massacre ended when Ryan turned the gun on himself after police had cornered him in the local school.

Today in 1820, the domineering Queen Caroline (the wife of George IV) went on trial in the House of Lords. The king was hoping to divorce her, but he was to be bitterly disappointed.

Today's births and deaths...
Blaise Pascal, philosopher and mathematician, died in 1662.
James Watt, who developed the first successful steam engines, died today in 1819.
Auguste Lumière, pioneer of movie films, was born in France, 1862.
Orville Wright, the first man to fly in a heavier-than-air machine, was born today in 1871.

AUG 20

On this day in 1961, East German soldiers began building a five-foot high concrete wall through the centre of Berlin, dividing the city in two. The Berlin Wall, which still stands, was built to prevent citizens from communist East Germany escaping to the West.

Emily Brontë, the author of *Wuthering Heights,* was born today in 1818.

Died on this day…
General William Booth, founder of the Salvation Army, died in 1912. His funeral procession through London was bigger than the procession for the Duke of Wellington.
Groucho Marx, the Marx Brother with the moustache. Groucho died in Santa Monica, California, in 1977. One of his most famous lines…

> Send two dozen roses to Room 424 and put 'Emily, I love you' on the back of the bill.

AUG 21

The film *Mary Poppins* was first seen by an invited audience in Hollywood, on this day in 1964.

On this day in 1968, Eastern Bloc tanks crossed the frontier into Czechoslovakia and crushed what was known as 'the Prague Spring'. Czech society had been becoming more liberal (people were wearing jeans and listening to pop music) and so the alarmed Russians put a stop to it all. Amidst massive protests, Russian tanks rolled into Prague and hundreds were arrested.

Today's birthdays…
Barry Norman, film critic and television broadcaster. Barry was born in 1933.

King William IV, affectionately known by his subjects as 'Silly Billy'. Bill was born in 1765.

On this day in 1940, **Leon Trotsky**, one of the original leaders of the Russian Revolution was assassinated in Mexico on the direct order of Stalin. Ramon Mercader, pretending to be a supporter of Trotsky, buried an ice-pick in Trotsky's skull.

AUG 22

Today in 1911, the world's most famous painting, the *Mona Lisa* by Leonardo da Vinci, was stolen from the Louvre in Paris. The painting was missing until its recovery over two years later in Florence. The thief was eventually sentenced to a year in prison.

On this day in 1485, the Battle of Bosworth Field took place in England. **King Richard III** was killed by the soldiers of Henry Tudor, who became Henry VII and started the Tudor line of monarchs. Henry's son was Henry VIII, and his grand-daughter was Elizabeth I.

On 22 August 1741, the composer George Handel began to work on a new piece of music. He finished it on 14 September, and decided to call it *The Messiah*.

Mr William Kendall successfully swam across the deadly rapids below Niagara Falls - with the aid of a cork vest. Several swimmers had died in the attempt before his crossing, which happened on this day in 1886.

The Red Cross was founded today in 1864.

The first public television broadcasts were transmitted in Britain on this day in 1932.

22 August is a birthday for **Steve Davies**, snooker supremo. Steve was born today in 1957.

AUG 23

On this day in 1926, **Rudolf Valentino**, the glamorous silent movie star, tragically died in New York. Only 31, his death caused hysteria worldwide among his female fans. Several of them committed suicide.

She Loves You, the Beatles single, was released today in 1963.

The night of 23 August was

the first night of the Blitz in London, during World War 2 in 1940. Bombers from the German Luftwaffe pounded London, causing widespread death and destruction.

Born today: **King Louis XVI** of France, in 1754. King Louis had his head removed during an encounter with a guillotine in the French Revolution just 39 years later.

AUG 24

On this day in AD79, the Roman seaside town of Pompeii was buried in volcanic ash and molten lava as nearby Mt Vesuvius erupted. Over 2,000 people died. The ruins of Pompeii, preserved in the lava, were discovered in 1748 and can still be seen.

On 24 August 1814, British soldiers captured the city of Washington during the British-American War. At 11pm, they arrived at the President's House. The place was deserted, but a massive dinner was laid out for 40 people. After eating and toasting King George and the US President, the soldiers set fire to the building. The house was later painted white to hide the scorch marks, which gave it its name, the White House.

The Massacre of St Bartholomew's in Paris took place on 24 August 1572. Large numbers of Protestants were killed by Catholics in widespread religious persecution.

On this day in the year 410, Rome fell to Alaric and the Goths, who sacked the city. This event marked the end of the once-mighty Roman Empire.

King Henry VII of Germany was poisoned on this day in 1313 as he received communion from a priest. The priest slipped him a poisoned wafer.

William Wilberforce, the campaigner against slavery, was born on this day in 1759.

AUG 25

At 10.41am, on 25 August 1875, Captain Matthew Webb staggered ashore at Calais Sands after a 21 hour 45 minute swim from Dover. He was the first man to swim the English Channel without a lifejacket.

On this day in 1944, Paris was liberated from the Nazis, after four years of occupation. Hitler had given orders that the Germans should destroy Paris rather than surrender, but the general in charge refused to do so.

Died on this day...
Pliny the Elder, the Roman scientist and historian, was killed in AD79 at Pompeii when the volcano Vesuvius erupted (see yesterday).
Sir William Herschel, who discovered the planet Uranus. Died in 1822.
Sir Henry Morgan, the buccaneer who became Lieutenant-Governor of Jamaica. He died in Jamaica, 1688.

AUG 26

26 August 1883: The volcanic island of Krakatoa in Java began to erupt. At 1pm there was a series of explosions every few minutes. At 2pm, a thick black cloud of volcanic ash descended. At 3pm, visibility was down to nil over a 50-mile radius around Krakatoa. The darkness was to last 57 hours. Read tomorrow for the next gripping installment...

The first book in JRR Tolkien's *The Lord of the Rings* was published in London on this day in 1954.

Born today...
Prince Albert, German

husband of Queen Victoria. Born in Bavaria, 1819. Albert introduced the Christmas tree (*with* baubles) to Britain.
Joseph Montgolfier, the first balloonist, was born in France, 1740.

Sir Francis Chichester, the first man to complete a solo voyage around the world, died today in 1972.

On this day in 55BC, the Romans under the leadership of Julius Caesar invaded Britain. Caesar later remarked about the invasion...

I came, I saw, I conquered.

AUG 27

27 August 1883: At 10.02pm 11 square miles of land on Krakatoa island collapsed into the volcano's central chamber. The sea roared in, causing the biggest explosion ever heard by humankind. The roar was heard as far away as Australia and the Indian Ocean. 36,417 people died in the series of massive waves that followed.

Fifty years after it was founded by the Dutch, the American city of New Amsterdam was captured by the British Colonel Nichols on this day in 1664. The city was renamed New York, after the Duke of York, who was given the city by King Charles II.

Martin Doyle became the last person in Britain to be hanged for *attempted* murder, today in 1861.

Today's birthdays...
Mother Teresa, who works with the poor and dying in Calcutta, was born today in 1910.
Confucius, the famous Chinese philosopher. He was born in 551BC.
Hegel, the not-quite-so-famous German philosopher. Born in 1770.
Lyndon Baines Johnson, the 36th President of the United States. He was made president when Kennedy was assassinated. Born in Texas, 1908.
Donald Bradman, the Australian cricketer. Also born in 1908.

AUG 28

Today is St Augustine's Day (he died this day in AD430). Augustine was the first-known person to be able to read to himself without moving his lips.

Born today: **Leo Tolstoy**, the Russian author of *War and Peace*. Born in 1828.

Died today: **Louis Pasteur**, father of pasteurized milk. Died in 1895.

On this day in 1963, Martin Luther King gave his famous 'I have a dream' speech at the Civil Rights demonstration in Washington. He told the

200,000 peaceful demonstrators...

> I have a dream that the sons of former slaves and the sons of former slave owners will sit together at the table of brotherhood.

The act of Parliament to abolish slavery throughout the British colonies was passed on this day in 1833. Parliament agreed to pay £20 million in compensation to the slave-owners.

AUG 29

On this day in 1883, 'the Ashes' trophy was instituted in cricket. The trophy consists of an urn containing the ashes of the stumps and bails used in the England-Australia test match in 1883. The winners of modern England-Australia

tests hold the ashes, although they are never removed from Lord's cricket ground.

The *Royal George*, a British man-of-war, capsized today in 1782 while carrying out repairs off Spithead. Six hundred of its crew and passengers were drowned.

The *Graf Zeppelin* airship

178

completed its circumnavigation of the globe on this day in 1929.

Michael Jackson was born on this day in 1958.

Revd William Archibald Spooner died on this day in 1930. Revd Spooner was the creator of spoonerisms (where the first letters of two words are switched). His jumbling up of words was accidental, but hilarious. He once announced a hymn as...

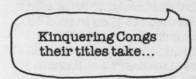

Kinquering Congs their titles take...

AUG 30

On this day in 1941, during World War 2, Nazi troops began the siege of Stalingrad. The bombardment of the city lasted for 880 days, killing an estimated 1.5 million people. The death toll made this the bloodiest-known siege in history.

Today is a 'Dismal Day' - it was considered to be an unlucky day in medieval England.

Today in 1968, the single *Hey Jude* was released by the Beatles.

On this day in 1878, a gigantic waterspout (the watery equivalent of a tornado) destroyed the town of Miskolcz in Hungary. Hundreds of people were killed.

Bubonic plague broke out in Glasgow on this day in 1900.

The first British tramway became operational in Birkenhead today in 1860.

Born today: **Mary Shelley**, who eloped with the poet Shelley when she was 17, and later wrote the horror story *Frankenstein*. Mary was born this day in 1797.

AUG 31

On this day in 1888, Jack the Ripper, the Victorian murderer, first struck in London. **Mary Ann Nichols** became his first victim in Whitechapel. He went on to murder four other women, and his identity has never been discovered.

Work started today in 1857 on the first tunnel under the Alps. The tunnel, connecting Savoy and Piedmont, was 7.5 miles long.

This day in 1900 saw the arrival from Atlanta, Georgia, of the first bottles of Coca-Cola in Britain. The few people who tasted it liked it. Coca-Cola has been here ever since.

Died today...
John Bunyan, the tinker from Bedford, who went on to write the classic *Pilgrim's Progress*. He died in 1688. **King Henry V**, in 1422. Henry was a great warrior-hero, and during his reign English archers gained their reputation as the best in Europe.

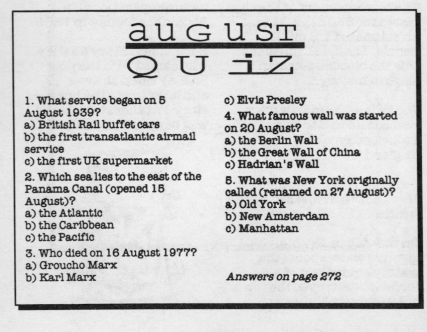

august QUIZ

1. What service began on 5 August 1939?
a) British Rail buffet cars
b) the first transatlantic airmail service
c) the first UK supermarket

2. Which sea lies to the east of the Panama Canal (opened 15 August)?
a) the Atlantic
b) the Caribbean
c) the Pacific

3. Who died on 16 August 1977?
a) Groucho Marx
b) Karl Marx

c) Elvis Presley

4. What famous wall was started on 20 August?
a) the Berlin Wall
b) the Great Wall of China
c) Hadrian's Wall

5. What was New York originally called (renamed on 27 August)?
a) Old York
b) New Amsterdam
c) Manhattan

Answers on page 272

SEPTEMBER

Name

The word September literally means *seventh month*. In ancient Rome, this was the seventh month of the year, until Julius Caesar adjusted the calendar by adding two new months - January and February. Even though September had become the ninth month, the Romans stuck with its old name.

They did the same with October, November and December, which are named after the numbers eight, nine and ten. These ancient names for our months have lasted over 2,000 years.

Red Letter Days

• 3 September is Crmwell's Day
• 23 September is the Autumn Equinox

SEPT 1

Just before 1 am on 1 September 1985, the wreck of the *Titanic* was discovered on the sea bed, lying in 12,460 feet of water. The ship had sunk with the loss of 1,500 lives 73 years earlier. The sea floor was littered with wine bottles, saucepans, spoons, safes, shoes, boilers, and the two halves of the ship itself.

On this day in 1939, at 5.45am, Nazi Germany launched a blitzkrieg attack on Poland. By 29 September, Warsaw was in Nazi hands and Poland had ceased to exist as an independent state. The invasion sparked off World War 2.

Edgar Rice Borroughs, the author of *Tarzan of the Apes*, and the other Tarzan stories, was born in Chicago on this day in 1875.

Died today...
Louis XIV, flamboyant King of France, known as 'the Sun King'. He was famous for his battles and his lovers. All the fun came to an end on this day in 1715.
Pope Adrian IV, the only English pope so far. His real name was Nicholas Breakspear. Died in 1159.

SEPT 2

2 September 1666: At 2am, a fire broke out when the oven door was left open in Farriner's Bakehouse in Pudding Lane, London. The smoke awoke the baker's servant, who raised the alarm. But it was already too late. The Great Fire of London had begun. By 3am London's Lord Mayor was awoken to be told the news. The fire was to rage over the next five days.

On this day in 1939, Britain's population went onto a war-footing. The

National Service Bill came into force, making 19-41 year-old men eligible to be called up into the armed forces.

Two deaths occurred on this day...
Percy Shaw, the man who invented Cat's eyes to mark the centre of roads at night, died today in 1976.
Mark Antony, famous as a Roman general and also as the lover of the Egyptian Queen Cleopatra. He lost the Battle of Actium, took it badly and committed suicide in 31BC.

SEPT 3

September 3rd -13th 1752 never happened in England. The calendar was adjusted to a new, more accurate system, and 11 days had to be 'lost' to catch up. So the day after 2nd September was to be called 14th September. This caused a lot of confusion, and many people were sure that their lives had been shortened by 11 days.

Today is a 'Dismal Day'. In medieval times, this day was believed to be unlucky.

On this day in 1939, Britain and France declared war on Germany. World War 2 had begun.

Richard the Lion Heart (King Richard I) was crowned in Westminster Abbey on this day in 1189. During the service, a bat flew around the throne on which Richard was sitting. People felt that this was a bad omen, and riots did break out in the streets later in the day...

On this day, Oliver Cromwell won two battles: the Battle of Dunbar in 1650 and the Battle of Worcester in 1651. On the same day in 1658, he died.

Viking II soft-landed on the surface of Mars on this day in 1976. The probe transmitted colour pictures of the planet's surface and tested the soil for signs of life.

Ferdinand Porsche, the motor car engineer, was born today in 1875.

JRR Tolkien, author of *The Hobbit* and *The Lord of the Rings*, died today, 1973.

SEPT 4

On this day in 1666, St Paul's Cathedral went up in flames as the Great Fire raged through London. Its six acres of lead on the roofs melted, pouring down into the streets in torrents. Thirty-four other London churches also burned down that day. King Charles II was seen helping to put out fires, covered in ash and grime. The present St Paul's Cathedral was built on the ruins of the first.

The US swimmer Mark Spitz won his seventh Olympic gold medal on this day in 1972. He was the first person ever to win seven gold medals at the Olympics.

Robert Raikes, the founder of Sunday Schools, was born today in 1735.

And it was goodbye to...
Edvard Grieg, the Norwegian composer. He died today in 1907.
Albert Schweitzer, the missionary doctor who spent his life in Gabon, Africa. He was a doctor three times over - of music, medicine and theology. Died today in 1965.

SEPT 5

On 5 September 1901, the American President, **William McKinley**, was assassinated by a Polish anarchist, Leon Czolgosz, in New York. He died nine days later. His vice-president, Theodore Roosevelt, took over office.

The first train travelled through the newly-completed Severn Tunnel on this day in 1885. The tunnel, just under 4.5 miles in length, running beneath the River Severn, is the longest and deepest tunnel in Britain.

On this day in 1912, the bizarre American composer **John Cage** was born. He is particularly famous for a piece of 'music' entitled *4'33"*, in which musicians of any number with any instruments sit on a stage in total silence for four minutes 33 seconds exactly. The audience is meant to listen appreciatively to any noises (coughing, nose-blowing, etc.) that occur.

The first play ever staged in the US was performed today in 1752. It was William Shakespeare's *The Merchant of Venice*.

On this day in 1972, an Arab terrorist group known as Black September, killed 11 members of the Israeli athletic team at the Olympic Games in Munich. Most of the team died when German police tried to free them while they were being held hostage at the airport.

SEPT 6

The first-ever circumnavigation of the Earth was completed on this day in 1522. Ferdinand Magellan had set out from San Lucar in Spain on 20 Sept 1519, but was killed two years later in the Philippines, during the homeward-bound journey across the Pacific. The *Vittoria* was the only ship of the original five that made it home.

On this day in 1666, the Great Fire of London was finally quenched. The fire (which had started on 2 September) destroyed 88 churches, St Paul's Cathedral, the city gates, the Guildhall, over 13,000 houses and 400 streets. But amazingly only eight people were reported to have died.

On this day in 1651, Charles II was forced to hide up an oak tree in Boscobel Wood near Worcester while soldiers searched for him below. He had just lost the Battle of Worcester to Oliver Cromwell and the Roundheads. At one point, Charles fell asleep in the tree and had to be woken in case he snored or fell off his branch.

SEPT 7

On this day in 1838, a British steamer travelling from Hull to Dundee, the *Forfarshire*, was wrecked in a violent storm. James Darling, a nearby lighthouse-keeper, and his daughter Grace, rowed through monstrous seas to save nine of the men from the doomed ship. Grace was awarded a medal for her heroism.

On 7 September 1533, Henry VIII's wife, Anne Boleyn, gave birth to her first child. Henry was bitterly disappointed that it was not a son. But the girl grew up to become **Queen Elizabeth I.** She never set foot outside England.

President Pinochet of Chile and his wife narrowly escaped an assassination attempt while travelling in their presidential car, today in 1986. They put their escape down to the protection of the Virgin Mary, whose image they claimed was formed by the bullet-holes in the car's protective shield.

Born on this day...
Buddy Holly, the rock'n'roller who sang *That'll be the Day* and *Peggy Sue*. Born in 1938.
Laura Ashley, Welsh fabric designer. Born in Merthyr Tydfil 1925.

SEPT 8

On this day in the year AD70, Jerusalem was captured, sacked and burnt by the Roman siege troops under the command of General Titus. The Jewish Temple was destroyed, never to be rebuilt, and the Jews who were left alive were driven from the city.

On this day in 1900, a hurricane in the Caribbean dropped an estimated 2,000 million tons of rain into the sea. The hurricane caused a tidal wave to sweep ashore at Galveston, Texas. 4,500 people were killed.

Today's birthdays include...
Peter Sellers (born Richard Henry Sellers), the comic actor who started his career as one of the Goons and ended it in the *Pink Panther* films. Born in 1925.
Anton Dvorák, the Czech composer who wrote the *New World Symphony*. Born near Prague in 1841.

The first V2 rocket - Hitler's secret weapon - exploded on Chiswick in London today in 1944. Each V2 carried one ton of explosives and impacted at 3,000mph from a height of 50 miles.

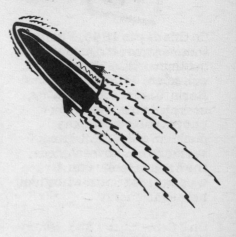

SEPT 9

On this day in 1981, the guillotine was abolished as a form of capital punishment in France.

Today in 1776, the American Congress declared that the 13 colonies were to be called the 'United States of America'. The colonies were in revolt against British rule, and this was the first time they were given this name.

The first British airmail letters were sent today in 1911 from Hendon to Windsor.

Died today...
Chairman Mao, the leader of the Chinese communist revolution, and author of the once much-read *Little Red Book*. Mao died in 1976.
William the Conqueror, who defeated the English at the Battle of Hastings in 1066, and who ordered the *Domesday Book*. William died in 1087 after falling off his horse in Rouen, France.

SEPT 10

On this day in 1945, Vidkun Quisling was sentenced to death in Oslo. A Norwegian politician, he had helped the Nazis to invade his country, and Hitler made him the puppet ruler of Norway during World War 2. His surname has now entered the English language. A quisling is a traitor who gives help to an enemy.

Arnold Palmer, the American golfer was born in Pennsylvania today in 1929.

Died on this day: **Mary Wollstonecraft**, an early feminist and the author of *Vindication of the Rights of Woman*. She died in 1797. She once said...

I do not wish women to have power over men; but over themselves.

SEPT 11

On this day in 1978, Bulgarian defector Georgi Markov was waiting for a bus at the bus stop on Waterloo Bridge in London. An innocent-looking passer-by suddenly jabbed him in the leg with a poison-tipped umbrella. Four days later Markov died in hospital despite the best efforts of the doctors. Bulgaria does not like defectors.

The first episode of *Danger Man* starring Patrick McGoohan was broadcast on television on this day in 1960.

DH Lawrence, the controversial author of *Lady Chatterley's Lover,* was born near Nottingham today in 1885.

President Allende of Chile was killed today in 1973, when a CIA-backed army coup overthrew the Marxist government. Thousands of people were rounded up by the military for interrogation. Many of them were never seen again.

On this day in 1940, four French schoolboys squeezed into a dark cave opening between the roots of a dead tree in Lascaux, France. They discovered a network of caves covered with Ice-Age paintings of bulls, horses and other animals. The caves and their priceless paintings had been forgotten for about 17,000 years.

Today marks a dark event in history: *The Monkees* LP was released in the US in 1966.

Cleopatra's Needle was erected on the Thames Embankment in London on this day in 1878. Weighing 186 tons, the Egyptian obelisk is 3,500 years old. The Needle had been shipped to Britain from Alexandria. This was its second move, as the Emperor Augustus had had it moved to Alexandria in 23BC.

Napoleon reached his moment of triumph over Russia on this day in 1812. He entered the deserted city of Moscow, which had surrendered before the French invasion. But during the evening, the Russians unbelievably started to set light to their own city. Napoleon was eventually forced by the flames to leave, which started off his disastrous retreat from Russia.

Steve Biko, the black civil rights leader, died on this day in 1977 six days after South African police took him into custody. The police claimed he had committed suicide, but he was clearly murdered.

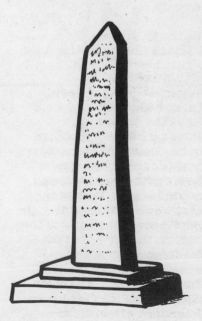

SEPT 13

On this day in 1959, the Soviet space probe, *Luna 2*, crashed onto the surface of the Moon just after 2 minutes past 9pm. It was the first man-made object to reach another celestial body. To commemorate the event, the probe contained a shock-resistant metal ball inscribed with the arms of the Soviet Union. The impact must have been violent: *Luna 2* was travelling at 7,500 mph as it hit the Moon (or 2 miles per second).

Died on this day...
W Heath Robinson, the

English cartoonist who drew fantastic contraptions designed to do the simplest tasks. He died in 1944. **James Wolfe**, the British general, who died trying to capture Quebec in 1759.

SEPT 14

On this day in 1854, the Crimean War began. It was fought between Russia and an alliance of France, Britain and Turkey.

The Gregorian Calendar came into use in Britain on this day in 1752. The old calendar (called the 'Julian Calendar', after Julius

Caesar) had been inaccurate, which meant that the dates were out of step with the seasons. Switching to the new calendar meant losing 11 days, so the date before 14 September in the year 1752 was 2 September. If you can follow that, you deserve a gold Blue Peter badge!

The following gasped their last today...
Dante Alighieri, the Italian

poet whose most famous book was the *Inferno*. He died in 1321 at Ravenna.
St Cyprian, who was martyred in AD258.
John of Chrysostom, one of the early church's red-hot preachers. Died in AD407.
The Duke of Wellington, known as 'the Iron Duke'. He won the Battle of Waterloo and later became Prime Minister. Wellington died in 1852. His last words were...

> Do you know where the apothecary lives? Then send and let him know that I should like to see him. I don't feel quite well and I will lie still till he comes.

SEPT 15

Today in 1784 saw the first ascent by balloon in Britain. The balloon's pilot, Vincent Lunardi took to the sky at Moorfields in London.

On this day in 1916, tanks were used in warfare for the first time at the Battle of the Somme, during World War 1. Thirty-six tanks went into action, terrorizing the German troops as they lumbered across the trenches. Each tank weighed 30 tons and nipped along at 4mph.

William Huskisson, a Victorian politician, was killed today in 1830 when he fell in the path of a moving steam engine (George Stephenson's *Rocket*) at the opening of the Liverpool and Manchester Railway. His leg was severed and he died later in the day. He was the first railway fatality.

Agatha Christie, the English crime writer, was born today in 1890.

Isambard Kingdom Brunel, the Victorian engineer who designed tunnels, bridges, ships and railways, died on this day, 1859.

191

SEPT 16

On this day in 1861, Post Office savings banks were first introduced in Britain.

Apart from that piece of exciting news, there are only two deaths to report for 16 September...

Daniel Gabriel Fahrenheit. The fahrenheit scale of temperature was named after him. Died in 1736.
Tomás de Torquemada, Inquisitor-General of the Spanish Inquisition. Under his direction, over 2,000 'heretics' were burnt at the stake. Torquemada died in 1498.

SEPT 17

Today's Earth-shattering news: The International Potato Exhibition opened on this day in 1879 at the Crystal Palace.

Today's birthdays...

Stirling Moss, motor racing champion, born in 1929.
Francis Chichester, the world's first solo round-the-world yachtsman. Chichester was born in 1901.

Fashion designer **Laura Ashley** died today in 1985 after falling downstairs at her home.

SEPT 18

British and Turkish troops met today in 1918 at the Battle of Megiddo in Palestine. Both sides must have been a bit nervous. Megiddo gives its name in the Bible to Armageddon, where it is believed that the final battle of all time will be fought.

Today in 1851 saw the first publication of the world-famous *New York Times*.

Happy birthday to...
Samuel Johnson, 18th-century wit and writer. Sam was born today in Lichfield, 1709.

Greta Garbo, one of Hollywood's first film stars, was born today in 1905.

The rock musician **Jimi Hendrix** died of a drug overdose on this day in 1970.

SEPT 19

Mickey Mouse made his first appearance in the Walt Disney film *Steamboat Willie* on this day in 1928.

Born today...
George Cadbury, the British chocolate maker. He was born in 1839.
William Golding, the author of *The Lord of the Flies* and other novels. Born in Cornwall, 1911.

Died today...
Thomas Barnardo, who founded the Dr Barnardo's Homes for homeless children in the 19th century. He died today in 1905.
Chester Carlson, who invented the Xerox photocopying process. Died in 1968.

SEPT 20

The 'Long Island Express', a 121-mph hurricane, ravaged New Hampshire in the US on this day in 1938. The steeple of the church in Dublin, New Hampshire, was upended and came down through the roof, skewering the pew where the minister's wife usually sat.

Salisbury Cathedral was consecrated on this day in 1258. Its spire, at 404 feet, is the highest church spire in Britain.

Today's births...
Prince Arthur, the first son of King Henry VII, in 1486. Henry called his son Arthur so that they would see him as a new King Arthur. Sadly, Arthur died young and was never crowned king.

Sophia Loren, the Italian film actress, was born on this day in 1934.

Samuel Johnson, the 18th-century wit and man of letters, coined one of his famous quotes today in 1777...

When a man is tired of London, he is tired of life...

SEPT 21

Today is a 'Dismal Day'. In medieval England, this day (and 23 others throughout the year) was believed to be unlucky.

Today is St Matthew's Day.

Matthew is famous for *Matthew's Gospel*, an account of the life of Jesus Christ.

The original Western movie, *Kit Carson*, was first screened in America on this day in 1903. The movie was just 21 minutes long.

On 21 September 1327, **King Edward II** was cruelly

murdered with a red-hot poker in the dungeon of Berkeley Castle. His wife, Isabella, had engineered his fate.

Stonehenge was sold on this day in 1915 along with 30 acres of land to a Mr CH Chubb for £6,600.

Today's birthday persons...

Simon Mayo. Yes, folks, this is *the* day. Born in 1958.
Owain Glyndwr, Welsh freedom fighter, died today in 1415.
Gustav Holst, the composer who wrote *The Planets Suite*. Born in 1874.
HG Wells, the author of *The Time Machine* and other scientific novels. Born in 1866.

SEPT
22

On this day in 1964, the James Bond film *Goldfinger* was premiered in Leicester Square, London.

22 September 1927 saw one of the most controversial world heavyweight boxing fights ever. The reigning champion Jack Tunney won the contest even though he was on the canvas for a full 15 seconds during the seventh round. Former champion Jack Dempsey was furious.

Horace Walpole, Britain's first Prime Minister, moved into 10 Downing Street on this day in 1735. From this date, No. 10 became the residence of Prime Ministers.

Solidarity, Poland's first free trade union, was founded in Gdansk shipyard on this day in 1980. Its leader was Lech Walesa.

On this day in 1761, George III was crowned king. During the coronation banquet, the largest jewel fell out of the king's crown. When Britain lost its American colonies 20 years later, many people felt that the dropping jewel had been an omen.

SEPT 23

The planet Neptune was discovered today in 1846 by an astronomer in Berlin. Neptune takes 165 years to orbit the Sun. If you drove a car at 70mph towards the planet, it would take you 4,500 years to arrive...

Today is the Autumnal Equinox. As the sun crosses the equator on its way south, day and night are exactly equal on this day.

The George Cross was instituted on this day in 1940. The medal is the highest award that civilians can receive for acts of courage in the face of danger.

The first Roman Emperor, **Augustus**, was born today in 63BC. The month of August is named after him. Also born today was **Bruce Springsteen**. 'The Boss' was born in 1949.

Sigmund Freud, the father of psychoanalysis, died in London on this day in 1939. Freud, who was Jewish, had been forced by the Gestapo to leave his home in Vienna for the safety of England. When his books were publicly burned by the Nazis, along with books by Albert Einstein, Freud remarked...

> At least I burn in the best of company.

SEPT 24

On this day in 1852, the first dirigible (a rigid airship) made its maiden flight. The 144-foot long ship flew the few miles from Paris to Trappes, piloted by Henri Giffard. Powered by steam, the airship shot along at 6mph.

During World War 1, a bomb-dropping German Zeppelin was shot down in Essex tonight in 1916. The German crew were arrested by a single policeman who had just put his trousers on after being awoken by the blast.

Today's birthdays...
Horace Walpole, gothic novelist and first British Prime Minister. Horace was

born in 1717.
F Scott Fitzgerald, the American author who wrote *The Great Gatsby*. Born in Minnesota, 1896.

SEPT 25

On this day in 1066, **Harald Hardrada**, King of Norway, was defeated by King Harold II of England at the Battle of Stamford Bridge. Only 19 days later, King Harold was killed at the Battle of Hastings.

25 September is a date that should be printed right through a stick of rock. The foundation stone for Blackpool Tower was laid on this day in 1891.

Today marks the first-ever mention of an Englishman drinking 'a cup of tea'. Samuel Pepys (the famous diarist) reported drinking the new brew on this day in 1660. Tea was quickly adopted as the national drink.

The unfortunately-named Battle of Loos started on this day in 1915. Perhaps the queues had become too long...

From today in 1956, you could phone up your grandmother in America. The transatlantic telephone service went into operation, via a cable laid on the Atlantic Ocean bed.

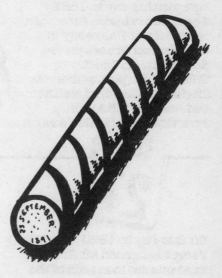

SEPT 26

On this day in 1934, the biggest ship in the world (at that time) was launched at Clydeside by Queen Mary, wife of George V. The *Queen Mary* was named after her.

Today's birthday boys...
Sir Barnes Neville Wallis, the inventor of the dambuster bombs used during World War 2. He was born on this day in 1887.
George Gershwin, American composer of *Rhapsody in Blue* and other jazz pieces. Born today in 1898.
TS Eliot, the poet who wrote *The Waste Land*, as well as *Old Possum's Book of Practical Cats* (which was used in the musical *Cats*). Born in Missouri, 1888.

Daniel Boone, the American pioneer who explored Kentucky, died on this day in 1820.

SEPT 27

On this day in 1829, a Dr JJ Parrot ascended Mt Ararat in Armenia, in search of the remains of Noah's Ark.

The Stockton and Darlington Railway, constructed by George Stephenson, was opened to passengers today in 1825. It was the world's first railway, and its trains travelled at the terrifying speed of 25-35mph.

The world's biggest ship of the time, the *Queen Elizabeth* was launched today in 1938. The ship started its slide into the waters of the Clyde too early, but the Queen managed to lob a bottle of bubbly at it just in time.

SEPT 28

On this day in 1066, Duke William of Normandy (later called William the Conqueror) landed in England at Pevensey, Sussex. He had come to do battle with King Harold II for the English throne. As he stepped from his ship, William fell flat on his face on the beach, which was seen as a bad omen. Despite this, William went on to win the Battle of Hastings.

The Radio Times was first published on this day in 1923.

St Wenceslas, patron saint of Czechoslovakia (and star of the Christmas carol *Good King Wenceslas looked out...*) died on this day in the year 929.

Brigitte Bardot, the French film star, was born today in 1934. Her real name? Camille Javal.

Louis Pasteur, the man who gave us pasteurised milk, died on this day in 1895. Pasteur also pioneered vaccination techniques.

God Save the King was sung for the first time in the Drury Lane Theatre, London, on this day in 1745. England was threatened by a Scottish invasion at the time, so patriotism was running high. It later became the official National Anthem. Here's how it goes (in case you've forgotten)...

God save our gracious Queen,
Long live our noble Queen,
God save the Queen:
Send her victorious,
Happy and glorious,
Long to reign over us:
God save the Queen.

SEPT 29

29 September 1978: At 4.45am, **Pope John Paul I** was discovered dead in bed by the nun who had brought him his morning coffee for 19 years. He had been pope for just 33 days. Some suspect that he was poisoned, but the Catholic church strongly denies it.

Today in 1950 saw the first-ever broadcast of *Come Dancing*.

Britain's first police force commenced duty on this day in 1829. London's 1,200-strong Metropolitan Police were also known as 'Peelers' or 'Bobbies' after Sir Robert Peel, the Home Secretary who brought them into being.

Today's birthdays...
Miguel de Cervantes, the Spanish author who wrote *Don Quixote*. Born in 1547.
Horatio Nelson, the hero of the Battle of Trafalgar, was born today in Norfolk, 1758. He was the son of a Rector.
Jerry Lee Lewis, piano basher, US rock'n'roll singer and performer of *Great Balls of Fire*. Born today in 1935.
Lech Walesa, leader of the Polish trade union *Solidarity*. Born in 1943.

SEPT 30

On this day in 1938, the British Prime Minister, Neville Chamberlain, returned from Munich with a signed peace agreement with Adolf Hitler. He told the crowds that he had

achieved...

Peace for our time.

On the same day in 1938, the front page of the *Daily Express* proclaimed: '*The Daily Express* declares that Britain will not be involved in a European war this year, or next year either.' Eleven months later, World War 2 started.

The first episode of *Thunderbirds* hit British television screens today in 1965. The puppet characters included Scott Tracey and his brothers Virgil, Alan, Gordon and John, together with Lady Penelope and her cockney butler Parker. Parker drove her ladyship's pink Rolls Royce, *FAB 1*.

On 30 September 1955, **James Dean**, the film actor, was killed when his Porsche careered off the road near Los Angeles.

Süleyman the Magnificent became Sultan of the Turkish Ottoman Empire on this day in 1520. One of the greatest sultans, he was also known as *Commander of the Faithful, Protector of Jerusalem, Lord of Lords of the World* and *Shadow of God on Earth,* to name but a few...

Born today...
William Wrigley Jr., the man who made chewing gum popular worldwide. Born in Philadelphia, 1861.

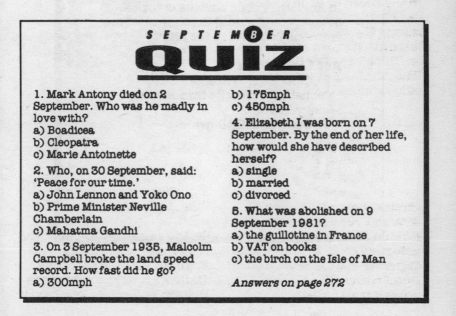

SEPTEMBER QUIZ

1. Mark Antony died on 2 September. Who was he madly in love with?
a) Boadicea
b) Cleopatra
c) Marie Antoinette

2. Who, on 30 September, said: 'Peace for our time.'
a) John Lennon and Yoko Ono
b) Prime Minister Neville Chamberlain
c) Mahatma Gandhi

3. On 3 September 1935, Malcolm Campbell broke the land speed record. How fast did he go?
a) 300mph
b) 175mph
c) 450mph

4. Elizabeth I was born on 7 September. By the end of her life, how would she have described herself?
a) single
b) married
c) divorced

5. What was abolished on 9 September 1981?
a) the guillotine in France
b) VAT on books
c) the birch on the Isle of Man

Answers on page 272

OCTOBER

Name
October was once the eighth month of the Roman year, and its name literally means *eighth month*. This was in the days when there were only ten months in the year.

In English, words such as octopus, octave, octagon and October all come from the Latin word for *eight*.

Red Letter Days
• 21 October is Trafalgar Day, celebrating Nelson's famous sea victory in 1805
• 31 October is Hallowe'en

OCT 1

After two-and-a-half years of civil war in China, Mao Tse-tung proclaimed that the country was a Communist Republic, today in 1949.

The Model T Ford went on sale in the United States on this day in 1908. The Model T was the first car with a left-hand drive.

The *News of the World* first hit the streets today in 1843.

On this day in 1800, America secretly bought the present-day state of Louisiana (plus seven other states) from France. For $27 million, the US doubled in size. Louisiana is named after King Louis XIV, from the days when it was a French colony.

Today's famous birthdays...
Julie Andrews, star of *The Sound of Music* and *Mary Poppins*, was born in Walton-on-Thames in 1935.
Jimmy Carter, the peanut farmer who became America's 39th president, was born in 1924.

Lord Shaftesbury, the great reformer who made it illegal for young children to work in mines and factories, died on this day in 1885. The poor people of London turned out in mass for his funeral. One man in rags paid him this tribute...

> Our Earl's gone! God A'mighty knows he loved us, and we loved him. We shan't see his likes again...

OCT 2

Britain's very first submarine, the *Holland I*, was launched at Barrow this day in 1901.

On this day in 1187, the Muslim army of the legendary warrior Saladin captured Jerusalem from its Christian rulers. This event sparked off the Crusades and a tune or two from Chris de Burgh.

Crowds at Twickenham (now the home of English rugby) saw the first rugby match played there today in 1909.

Birthday persons for today... **Sting**, rock singer formerly with the Police. Sting was born on this day in 1950. **Graham Greene**, the English novelist who wrote *Brighton Rock* and other great novels. Graham was born in 1904. **King Richard III**, reputed to have murdered the princes in the Tower of London. Born at Fotheringay Castle, 1452. **Mahatma Gandhi**, the peaceful protester who won India's independence. Born in 1869. **Groucho Marx** was born in New York today in 1890. His real first name was Julius. Or as Groucho put it...

> No, Groucho is not my real name. I'm breaking it in for a friend.

OCT 3

On 3 October 1899, the Boer War started. The war was between Dutch settlers and was fought in South Africa. Shockingly, 26,000 women and children died in British concentration camps during this war.

On this day in 1906, the Morse signal SOS was first adopted as the official international distress signal in Berlin. The SOS signal (standing for 'Save Our Souls') gradually replaced the older CQD distress code.

Today is a 'Dismal Day'. In medieval England, this day was believed to be unlucky. There are 24 of these Dismal

Days in each year: two per month.

The first British atom bomb was detonated off the north-west coast of Australia on this day in 1952. The test at

OCT
4

the uninhabited Monte Bello Islands was watched by scientists and members of the armed forces.

St Francis of Assisi died this morning in 1226.

John Bowler, the hat-maker, today in 1850.

The space age began on this day in 1957 with the launch of *Sputnik I* by Russia. Sputnik I, a 22-inch ball that transmitted radio signals, was the first human-made object to be sent into orbit.

The first complete English-language Bible, translated by the Yorkshireman Miles Coverdale, rolled off the presses in Zurich on this day in 1535. The Bible was dedicated to Henry VIII.

Staying with the religious theme, the television series *The Saint*, starring Roger Moore as Simon Templar, was first broadcast on this day in 1962.

Today also marks the anniversary of the Bowler Hat. The round-topped hat, much loved by city gents, was created in London by

Born today...
Buster Keaton, the silent-film comedian who did his own stunts, falling off trains and hanging by a thread over waterfalls. Born in 1895.
Charlton Heston, the film star who starred in *Ben Hur*. Heston was born in 1924.

Died today...
Rembrandt, one of the great artists, died on this day in 1669.
Janis Joplin, the rock musician, 1970.

OCT 5

Today in 1969 saw the first broadcast of a new line in television comedy. *Monty Python's Flying Circus* began transmission at 11pm this night.

And now for something completely different...

On this day in 1793 (at the time of the French Revolution), the Revolutionary Calendar was decreed in Paris. There were to be 12 months of 30 days each, with 5 'additional' days to make up the year. Depressingly, five of the months were named after bad weather: Brumaire (foggy), Frimaire (frosty), Nivose (snowy), Pluviose (rainy) and Ventose (windy). Luckily for everyone, the idea never really caught on.

Today is a birthday for **Bob Geldof**. The Boomtown Rat turned fund-raiser for the Third World was born on this day in Dublin in 1954. Bob was awarded a knighthood in 1986 for his work with *Band Aid* and *Live Aid*.

OCT 6

Today in 1973 marked the beginning of the Yom Kippur War against Israel. Egypt and Syria launched their shock attack on Yom Kippur, the holiest date in the Jewish calendar.

On this day in 1536, **William Tyndale** was executed by strangling in Antwerp. His crime? He had translated the Bible into English and had copies smuggled into Britain. His final words were a prayer that Henry VIII would allow the Bible to be legally translated...

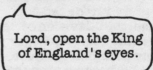

Lord, open the King of England's eyes.

The first episode of *Stingray* appeared on British television on this day in 1964. The all-puppet cast included Captain Troy

Tempest, Phones, and the gorgeous, green-haired Marina. The submarine Stingray was powered with an atomic motor, and viewers were given the warning...

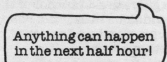

Anything can happen in the next half hour!

Born on this day...

Matteo Ricci, pioneering Jesuit missionary to China, 1552.

Thor Heyerdahl, who proved his theories about human migration with two voyages. In 1947 he sailed a balsa raft, the *Kon Tiki*, from Peru to the South Pacific Tuamoto Islands. And in 1970 he sailed the *Ra II*, a papyrus boat, from Africa to Barbados. Born in 1914.

OCT 7

7 October 1930: 44 passengers died when the world's largest airship, the British *R101*, crashed into a French hillside and exploded in a ball of flame. The airship had been drenched by rain, which weighed it down, making it difficult to steer.

The world's first car assembly line went into operation on this day in 1913. The Ford production line in Michigan saw one new car built every three hours, totalling 250,000 a year.

London's tallest building at the time, the Post Office Tower (now the Telecom Tower), was opened today in 1965. The Tower stands 620 feet tall and originally had a revolving restaurant on top.

President Gerald Ford made a spectacular gaffe on US television tonight in 1976. He insisted against all the facts that the Soviet Union does not dominate Eastern Europe.

The human race had its first-ever glimpse of the far side of the Moon on this day in 1959. The stunning pictures were beamed to Earth from the Soviet probe *Luna III*, which had gone into orbit around the Moon.

Clive James, the television broadcaster, was born on this day in Sydney, in 1939.

OCT 8

On 8 October 1871, the Great Fire of Chicago broke out, lasting for four days. By the time the fire died down on 11 October, 250 people had lost their lives in the flames, and 95,000 were left on the streets, having lost their homes and their possessions.

On this day in the year 451, the church Council of Chalcedon opened. The council hammered out what the church believed about who Jesus Christ was.

Jessie Jackson, the black American politician, was born today in 1941.

Died today...
Clement Attlee, Labour Prime Minister of Britain immediately after World War 2. He died in 1967.
Henry Fielding, the magistrate and author of the scandalous book, *Tom Jones*. People blamed a London earthquake soon after publication on the book. Fielding died in Lisbon in 1754. A quote from the book...

> His designs were strictly honourable, as the saying is: that is, to rob a lady of her fortune by way of marriage.

OCT 9

9 October 1963: Disaster struck the 870-foot high Vaiont Dam in the Italian Alps. A landslip on a hillside overlooking the lake plunged 260 million cubic metres of earth into the water, causing a massive wave to travel across the lake. The water spilt over the top of the dam, sending a 600-foot wall of water crashing down the valley beyond. 1,900 people were killed as alpine villages were simply washed off the map.

On this day in 1967, British motorists were stopped by police for the first time and asked to blow into a little plastic bag. The first breathalysers had arrived.

Born today…
Jacques Tati, the French film comedian, who created *Monsieur Hulot's Holiday*. Born in 1908.
John Lennon, Beatle and musician in his own right, was born in Liverpool this day, 1940.

Died today…
Che Guevara, the Bolivian revolutionary, shot dead by Bolivian troops in 1967.
Jonathan Swift, the author of *Gulliver's Travels*, died in 1745.

OCT 10

On this day in 1897, Felix Hoffmann, a German chemist, succeeded in inventing aspirin in a laboratory. He was trying to find a pain-reliever for his poor old dad, who suffered from rheumatism. Aspirin went on to become one of the world's best-selling medicines.

The Panama Canal was opened on this day in 1913. A massive blast of dynamite, detonated by President Roosevelt pressing a button on his desk in the White House, cleared the final obstacle between the Atlantic and Pacific Oceans.

Today was a bad day for actors. Both **Yul Brynner** (star of *The Magnificent Seven* and other film greats) and **Orson Welles** (director and star of *Citizen Kane*) died on exactly the same day, 1985.

OCT 11

On this day in 1982, The *Mary Rose*, Henry VIII's flagship, was gently lifted out of the Solent mud, 437 years after she capsized and sank. The ship had sunk as Henry VIII watched from the shore, due to being too heavily laden.

Henry IV, who had just been proclaimed king, created 40 new knights this evening in 1399 in the Tower of London. The Order of the Bath (a form of knighthood) dates from this event.

George II was crowned on this day in 1727. George was the last British king to lead his soldiers into battle.

Today's birthdays...
Henry Heinz, the food magnate who started out with 57 varieties. Born in 1844.
Richard Burton, the Welsh actor who was married twice to Elizabeth Taylor. Born in 1925.

OCT 12

12 October 1984: At 2.54am, an IRA bomb tore apart the Grand Hotel in Brighton, where most of the cabinet were staying during the Conservative Party Conference. Three people were killed. Mrs Thatcher's hotel bathroom, where she had been just two minutes before the blast, was devastated by the 20lb bomb.

Edith Cavell, a British nurse, was executed by a German firing squad on this day in 1915. Edith's crime had been helping British and French soldiers to escape across the Belgian-Dutch border during World War 1. Her last words...

> I must have no hatred or bitterness towards anyone.

Today in 1216, King John lost the Crown Jewels in the estuary of the River Ouse. He was crossing the marshes at low tide in the mist, when the wagons carrying the treasure got lost and were swept out to sea by the rapidly-returning tide. John died a few days later.

Magnus Magnusson, broadcaster and presenter of *Mastermind*, was born on this day in 1929.

OCT 13

On this day in 1399, King Henry IV was crowned at Westminster Abbey with great splendour. He had forced King Richard II to resign his throne.

Gerald Ford was made vice-president of the United States by President Nixon on this day in 1973. Nixon's original vice-president, Spiro Agnew, had been forced to resign due to the Watergate scandal. When Nixon resigned the following August, Ford became president.

Today's birthdays...
Margaret Hilda Thatcher, Britain's first woman Prime Minister. Margaret was born in a grocer's shop in Grantham, 1925.
Paul Simon, the American singer and songwriter, originally part of Simon and Garfunkel. Simon is not only famous for his songs *Mrs Robinson* and *Bridge Over Troubled Water*, but also for his solo material - including the legendary *Graceland* album in 1986. He was born in New Jersey, 1941.

OCT 14

14 October 1066: William the Conqueror defeated King Harold II of England to win the Battle of Hastings. William, originally the Duke of Normandy, now became King of England.

On this day in 1947, Chuck Yeager, a US Air Force test pilot, broke the sound barrier. He was hurtling at 670mph in a Bell X1 rocket plane flying over Edwards Air Force Base, California. Yeager had broken two ribs in a moonlight horse ride two days earlier, but he cleverly concealed his injury to stop him from being scrubbed from the historic flight.

Today in 1829, George Stephenson's *Rocket* won the competition to be the steam engine first used on the Liverpool and Manchester railway. The competition was held at Rainhill Bridge, Manchester.

The 50p piece became part of British coinage on this day in 1970. It was Britain's first decimal coin.

Born today...
Cliff Richard (real name Harry Webb) was born in Lucknow, India, on this day in 1940.
Roger Moore, the film actor, was born this day in 1927.

Bing Crosby died while playing golf on this day in 1977..

OCT 15

On this day in 1917, the seductive female spy, **Mata Hari**, was executed in France. She had discovered masses of French wartime secrets from her military lovers, and then passed them on to the Germans. Mata Hari was originally a Dutch

dancer.

Just hours before he was due to be hanged for his Nazi war crimes, **Hermann Goering**, Hitler's right-hand man, committed suicide by swallowing a cyanide pill. The date: 15 October 1946.

Born on this day...
Florence Nightingale, who reformed standards in

hospitals and became known as 'the lady with the lamp' from her work among the wounded during the Crimean War. She was born in (and named after) Florence, in 1820.

PG Wodehouse, English author, and the creator of Jeeves, the typical English butler. Born in Guildford, 1881. From one of the 'Jeeves' books...

> I was so darned sorry for poor old corky that I hadn't the heart to touch my breakfast. I told Jeeves to drink it himself.

OCT 16

On this day in 1987, the worst storm of the century smashed its way through southern Britain. The small hurricane, with winds of up to 110mph, killed 17 people and uprooted millions of trees. A weather forecaster the previous night had laughed at a viewer's suggestion that there might be a hurricane.

Cardinal Karol Wojtyla of Poland was chosen to become Pope John Paul II on this day in 1978. He was the first non-Italian to be chosen as pope since 1542.

Today in 1846 marked the first use of anaesthetic during an operation. William Morton used ether to put a patient to sleep while a tumour was removed from the patient's neck. The operation took place at Massachusetts General Hospital in America. Before this time, patients simply had to lie still during operations.

Born today...
David Ben Gurion, Israel's first Prime Minister. Born in Poland, 1886.
Oscar Wilde, the 19th-century wit who wrote the play *The Importance of Being Earnest*. Born in Dublin, 1854.

Executed today...
Marie Antoinette, Queen of France, guillotined in 1793.
Bishops Latimer and Ridley, burnt at the stake for 'heresy' in 1555.

OCT 17

On this day in 1902, the first Cadillac car made in Detroit was sold in America.

On 17 October 1662, Charles II sold Dunkirk, which had been an English possession, to France.

Today's births...
Arthur Miller, the American playwright who wrote *Death of a Salesman*, and who married Marilyn Monroe. Arthur was born in 1915.
Rita Hayworth, the film actress, born in New York, 1918.

Frédéric Chopin, the Polish composer and virtuoso pianist, died in Paris today in 1849.

My other car's a Porsche!

OCT 18

Today is St Luke's Day. Luke was a doctor who wrote his version of the life of Christ, *Luke's Gospel*.

The Soviet probe *Venus IV* became the first craft to achieve a soft landing on another planet, this day in 1967. It sank slowly through Venus's thick atmosphere using a special parachute, and revealed that surface temperatures climb as high as 280°C and that the atmosphere is almost entirely carbon dioxide.

Born today...
Martina Navratilova, six times the winner of the Wimbledon singles title in tennis. Born in Prague, 1956.
Lee Harvey Oswald, the man who shot President Kennedy in 1963. Born today in 1939.

Died today...
Lord Palmerston, the Prime

Minister who was fond of sending in British gunboats when britons were threatened overseas. He died in 1865. His last words...

Die, my dear doctor? That's the last thing I shall do!

OCT 19

On this day in 1812, Napoleon and the French army began their retreat from Moscow. Harried by Russian soldiers and the bitter Russian winter, the retreat became a disaster for Napoleon. This day marked the beginning of the end for him.

Today in 1807, Sir Humphrey Davy, the English scientist, announced his discovery of a new metal, sodium. Sodium is the 11th atomic element.

King John, younger brother to Richard the Lion Heart, died of a fever today in 1216. John had hastened his death by greedily eating peaches and drinking cider a few days before.

OCT 20

The Sydney Opera House was opened today in 1973 by Queen Elizabeth II.

On this day in 1922, Lieutenant Harold Harris became the first man to avoid death by using a parachute.

Sir Christopher Wren was born today in 1632. Wren was the architect who designed the present St Paul's Cathedral in London after the old building was gutted in London's Great Fire of 1666.

Today in 1714, King George I was crowned in Westminster Abbey.

Grace Darling died today at the age of 27 in 1842. Grace, a lighthouse-keeper's daughter, rescued nine crew members from the wreck of the *Forfarshire* during a storm four years earlier.

OCT 21

21 October 1805: The Battle of Trafalgar was fought between the British and the French in 1805. At 12 noon, Admiral Lord Nelson sent the famous message to the whole British fleet...

> England expects that every man this day will do his duty.

Soon afterwards the fleets engaged, and French ships began to surrender. At 1.15pm, **Nelson**, on board the *Victory*, was mortally wounded in the shoulder by a French sniper, and was taken below decks to die. National rejoicing at the victory at Trafalgar was mixed with mourning for Nelson's death.

21 October 1966: Shortly after morning assembly at the village school in Aberfan, South Wales a coal tip slid down the hillside and buried the school, a row of houses and a farm. 144 people were killed in the black avalanche, 116 of them children. The minister for Wales said...

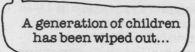

A generation of children has been wiped out...

Alfred Nobel, inventor of dynamite and founder of the Nobel prizes. Born in 1833.

Born today...
Samuel Taylor Coleridge, the romantic poet famous for his poem, *The Rime of the Ancient Mariner*. Born in 1772.

OCT 22

The world's first parachute drop was made on this day in 1797. André-Jacques Garnerin hopped out of a balloon at 6,000 feet, yanked open the chute and - lived!

Today is a 'Dismal Day'. It was believed to be an unlucky day in medieval times.

Chicago police got their man today in 1931. Al 'Scarface' Capone was the most powerful Chicago gangster, responsible for the St Valentine's Day Massacre of 1929. On this day he was jailed for 11 years - for tax dodging. The police couldn't make any more serious charges against him stick.

America's most notorious criminal was sent to its most notorious prison - Alcatraz.

Franz Liszt, the composer and pianist, was born in Hungary on this day in 1811. When only 11 years old, Beethoven admired his style of playing.

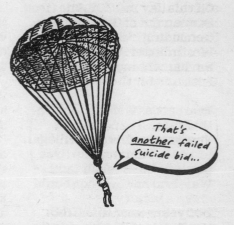

That's *another* failed suicide bid...

OCT
23

At 9am on 23 October 4004BC, God created the world. At least, that was the rough estimate according to the 17th-century Bishop James Ussher.

A dog in Buenos Aires caused three deaths as it fell from a 13th-floor balcony on this day in 1988. The dog inflicted a fatal blow as it landed on one woman. Another woman in the crowd that had gathered to watch was knocked over by a passing bus. A man who saw both deaths then had a heart attack. The dog walked away unharmed...

On this day in 1707, the first Parliament of Great Britain (excluding Ireland) sat in Westminster. The new Parliament incorporated Scotland for the first time.

Two battles were fought on this date...
The **Battle of Edge Hill** began in 1642. This was the first battle of the English Civil War, and neither side could claim a victory.
300 years later to the day, the **Battle of El Alamein** (in

World War 2) began in 1942. General Montgomery went on to defeat Field Marshall Rommel in this famous tank battle in the desert of Egypt.

Pele, the Brazillian footballer, was born today in 1940.

William Gilbert Grace, the famous Victorian cricketer, died today in 1915.

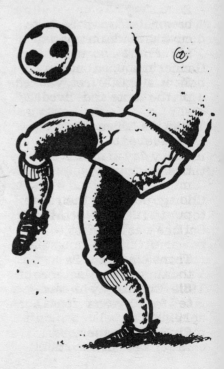

24 October 1929: This date is remembered as Black Thursday on New York's Wall Street. 13 million shares changed hands as the market crashed causing panic throughout the financial world. The Wall Street crash heralded the world-wide Depression era during the early 1930s.

On this day in 1901, Ann Edson Taylor climbed into a barrel padded with thick cushions. The barrel was sealed and pushed into the river just above Niagara Falls. Ann survived the plunge to tell reporters that she had done it to keep up with her mortgage repayments.

Clergymen who committed murder in England were no longer excused from punishment, from this day in 1513.

Three knights were born today...
Sir Robin Day, bow-tied television interviewer, born 1923.
Sir Fred Pontin, holiday camp creator, born 1906.

Sir Robert Sainsbury, supermarket boss, born 1906.

Bill Wyman of the Rolling Stones was also born today in 1941. He's not *Sir* Bill, at least, not yet...

Died today...
Tycho Brahe, the Danish astronomer who wore a metal nose to replace the one he lost in a duel. Died in 1601.
Pyotr Ilyich Tchaikovsky, composer of *The Nutcracker Suite* and *Swan Lake*. Died in St Petersburg, 1893.

OCT 25

Today is St Crispin's Day. St Crispin is the patron saint of shoemakers.

The Battle of Agincourt was fought between the English and French on this day in 1415. Many French soldiers fell down and could not get up again because of their heavy armour. They were killed by bare-footed English archers. King Henry V won an overwhelming victory for England.

The satirical magazine, *Private Eye*, was first published on this day in 1961.

Today in 1854 saw the Charge of the Light Brigade at the Battle of Balaclava. Lord Cardigan was ordered to charge the Russian guns with his horse-mounted cavalry. The 670 horsemen obeyed at once, even though the order was clearly ridiculous. Only 198 returned.

Born today...
Pablo Picasso, probably the greatest artist of the 20th century. Born in Spain, 1881.
Johann Strauss, composer of The *Blue Danube* waltz. Born in Vienna, 1825.

Died today...
Geoffrey Chaucer, who wrote the racy *Canterbury Tales*. He died in 1400.
William Hogarth, the satirical 18th-century engraver. Died 1764.

OCT 26

On this day in 1965, the four Beatles received their OBEs from the Queen at Buckingham Palace. Outside the palace gates, thousands of screaming fans waited for a glimpse of the Fab Four.

Two new plane services came into being on this day in

1958. Passengers could now choose between the New York-London jet service (run by BOAC) or the New York-Paris jet service (by Pan Am).

Victor Emmanuel was proclaimed the first King of Italy today in 1860.

Mahalia Jackson, the Gospel singer, was born in New Orleans on this day in 1911. **Bob Hoskins**, the film actor, was born today in 1942.

OCT 27

in Geneva. He was roasted alive for heresy in 1553.

Today's births...
John Cleese, comedy actor and former member of the *Monty Python* team, was born this day in 1939.
Captain James Cook, who went on to explore the Pacific Ocean in his ship, the *Eneavour*, and especially Australia's east coast. Jim was born in Yorkshire in 1728.
Isaac Singer, the inventor of the sewing machine. Isaac was born in New York, 1811.
Dylan Thomas, the Welsh poet, was born in Swansea today in 1914.

And today's deaths...
Richard Turner, the first teetotaller, died in 1846. He accidentally coined the phrase due to his stutter when speaking in public.
Michael Servetus had a not very enjoyable October 27th

OCT 28

On this day in 1886, the Statue of Liberty was unveiled in New York Harbour. The statue was a gift to America from the people of France. Built in France, it had been floated across the Atlantic.

Christopher Columbus discovered Cuba today in 1492. He was sure that he had reached the coast of Asia, not realizing that America and the Pacific Ocean were in the way.

Guiseppe Roncalli, an Italian farmer's son, was elected Pope John XXIII on this day in 1958. He remained pope until his death in 1963.

Alfred the Great, one of the best-loved Kings of England, died on this day in 901. King Alfred's crown was unique among English crowns. It had two bells attached to it.

OCT 29

Sir Walter Raleigh, the Elizabethan explorer who introduced tobacco to Britain, was beheaded today in 1618. Sir Walter had been imprioned in the Tower of London since Queen Elizabeth I had died, but he was let out for a last expedition to the Orinoco River in search of gold. The expedition failed abysmally, so his head rolled.

Also executed on this date, in 1901, was **Leon Czolgosz**. He went to the electric chair for the assassination of the American President, William McKinley.

Born today…

Edmund Halley, the astronomer who successfully predicted the return of Halley's comet. Born in 1656.

Paul Josef Goebbels, Hitler's propaganda minister. Born in 1897.

J Kemp Starley, the inventor of the safety bicycle (which is still in use) died today in 1901. His cycle replaced the penny-farthing and other models.

the first time.

The last Chinese Emperor, aged five, surrendered absolute power in China on this day in 1911. His declaration ended three centuries of rule by the Manchu dynasty.

On this day in 1905, aspirin went on sale in Britain for

King Henry VII was crowned in Westminster Abbey today in 1485. During the festivities, some scaffolding full of sightseers collapsed, but fortunately no one was injured.

Fyodor Dostoyevsky, the Russian novelist who wrote *The Brothers Karamazov*, was born on this day, 1821.

OCT 31

Today is the Eve of All Hallows (Hallowe'en). This is the last day of the old Celtic Year, when supernatural spirits were believed to be flying around. They knew this day as *Samian Eve*. Superstitions about spooky happenings on this day date back thousands of years.

On this day in 1517, Martin Luther nailed his 95 Theses (arguments against church abuses) to the door of the Castle Church in Wittenberg. This action started off the Protestant Reformation.

Harry Houdini, the American escapologist, died today in 1926. Harry prided himself on being able to take a punch in the stomach. He invited a visitor to his dressing room to punch him, but the visitor hit him before he was ready. He died of a burst appendix.

Walt Disney's film *Dumbo* was released today in 1941.

John Keats, the romantic poet, was born on this day in 1795.
Jimmy Saville was born today in 1926.

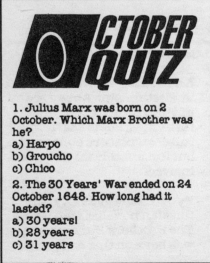

OCTOBER QUIZ

1. Julius Marx was born on 2 October. Which Marx Brother was he?
a) Harpo
b) Groucho
c) Chico

2. The 30 Years' War ended on 24 October 1648. How long had it lasted?
a) 30 years!
b) 28 years
c) 31 years

3. What was destroyed by fire on 16 October?
a) a copy of the *Mona Lisa*
b) the Queen Mary
c) the Houses of Parliament

4. What was discovered on 28 October 1492?
a) Cuba
b) the world's largest diamond
c) the Dodo

5. Margaret Thatcher was born on 13 October 1925. How old was she when she became Prime Minister?
a) 61
b) 57
c) 53

Answers on page 272

Name
November for the ancient Romans was the ninth month of the year, and that is what its name means. It has been the eleventh month since 44BC, but it has stubbornly kept its old name.

Red Letter Days
• 1 November is All Saints' Day
• 5 November is Guy Fawkes' Night, celebrating the foiled plot to blow up Parliament in 1605
• 17 November is Queen's Day, marking the day when Queen Elizabeth I came to the throne
• 30 November is St Andrew's Day - the patron saint of Scotland

NOV 1

Since the 8th century AD, today has been celebrated as All Saints' Day. For Celts, this was the first day of the new year, celebrated as the festival of *Samian*.

1 November 1755: At 9.30am, a series of violent earthquakes struck the city of Lisbon, in Spain. In three violent quakes, following quickly after each other, 17,000 of the city's 20,000 houses collapsed, killing an estimated 30,000 people. Many died as the cathedral collapsed on top of them.

On this day in 1959, the M1 was opened to traffic.

Spencer Perceval, the only British Prime Minister ever to have been assassinated, was born in London today in 1762.

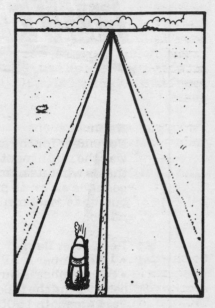

NOV 2

On this day in 1976, Jimmy Carter, former peanut farmer from Georgia, was elected the 38th President of the United States.

On the same date in 1930, Ras Tafari was crowned Emperor Haile Selassie of Abyssinia in Addis Ababa. Ras Tafari is the focus of Rastafarianism.

A solid gold bedstead was presented to Queen Victoria by the Maharajah of Cashmere on this day in 1859.

This day in 1903 saw the *Daily Mirror* presses roll for the first time.

The first crossword ever to appear in a British newspaper was published in the *Sunday Express* on this day in 1924.

On this day in 1960, a jury at the Old Bailey found that the novel *Lady Chatterley's Lover*, by DH Lawrence, was not obscene. The book had been banned in Britain for 30 years.

Two royals who met violent ends were born today...

King Edward V, born 1470. Edward was only 13 when he came to the throne, and he was deposed after three months by his uncle, Richard III. Edward and his brother were later murdered in the Tower of London.

Marie Antoinette, the Queen of France guillotined in the French Revolution. Born 1755.

NOV
3

On this day in 1957, the Russians launched their second satellite, *Sputnik II*. The craft carried the first-ever space traveller from Earth. She was a small Russian dog called Laika. Sadly, Laika never returned from her journey around the Earth.

On 3 November 1679, a comet was spotted heading towards the Earth. The comet gave us a near-miss, which caused panic and supersition throughout Europe. Everyone felt that terrible events were about to happen on Earth.

Lulu, the Scottish pop singer, was born on this day in 1958. Her real name is Marie McDonald Lawrie.

On this night in 1605, the Gunpowder Plot was uncovered in Westminster. King James was due to open Parliament on the 5th, and a number of catholic conspirators had tunnelled into the cellar below the House of Lords. Acting on a tip-off, a search was made of the cellar at midnight, and Guy Fawkes plus 36 barrels of gunpowder were discovered. Fawkes was executed the following January.

On this day in 1860, Abraham Lincoln was elected President of the United States. His election sparked off the American Civil War, over the issue of the abolition of slavery in the southern states.

Wilfred Owen, the famous poet of World War 1, was killed in action on this day in 1918. As he led his company across a canal, he was cut down by machine-gun fire. The war ended just seven days later.

Today in 1931, Mahatma Gandhi arrived at Buckingham Palace for an audience with the king - wearing only a loincloth and an old shawl. Gandhi was the leading figure in the Indian movement for independence from the British Empire. The King, Queen and Gandhi had a cup of tea together.

Died on this day...
The English Admiral, **John Benbow**, in 1702. Benbow, a popular hero, was killed in a battle with the French off Jamaica.
Felix Mendelssohn, the German composer. He died in 1847.

Today is a 'Dismal Day' - believed to be unlucky in the middle ages.

Tonight is Guy Fawkes' Night, when effigies of Guy Fawkes are still burnt on bonfires throughout Britain. It was on this day in 1605 that the news broke about the Gunpowder Plot (see 4

November). Guy Fawkes' old school in York has always refused to burn one of its old boys.

Today in 1956, the Soviet Red Army invaded Hungary and crushed a revolution that was taking place against Soviet rule. Tanks flattened houses in the search for snipers and the Hungarian government was arrested.

On this day in 1968, Richard Nixon was elected President of the United States. He remained President until 1974.

Art Garfunkel, of Simon and Garfunkel fame, was born this day in New York, 1941.

NOV 6

On this day in 1952, the world's first H-Bomb was exploded at Eniwetok Atoll, an island in the Pacific. In the explosion, the island completely disappeared. The H-Bomb used an Atom Bomb as a trigger to set off a massively bigger explosion.

Queen Victoria opened Blackfriars Bridge over the Thames in London on this day in 1869.

Today saw the birth of two inventors of musical instruments...
Adolphe Sax, the inventor of the saxophone, was born in Belgium today in 1814.
John Philip Sousa, the American composer and inventor of the sousaphone (a sort of massive tuba) was born today in 1854. Sousa is also famous for his military marches, one of which was used for the opening credits of *Monty Python's Flying Circus*.

7 November 1872: A ship was sighted west of Spain with its sails set, but steering erratically. The ship was the *Mary Celeste,* and was completely deserted. The crew of eight, plus the captain, his wife and two-year-old daughter had simply disappeared. The lifeboat was missing, but the ship was in good condition. The mystery of the Mary Celeste has never been solved.

A disastrous day in history. Not only was the Mary Celeste sighted, but Rolf Harris's single *Two Little Boys* was released!

The Russian Revolution took place on this day in 1917. The Bolsheviks (Russian communists) overthrew the Russian government and Lenin came to power. This date marks the beginning of modern Russian history. The revolution is called the 'October Revolution' because it took place in that month according to the old Russian calendar.

Today in 1919, Nancy Astor became Britain's first woman MP. Nancy Astor frequently clashed with Winston Churchill. On one occasion they had this exchange of views...

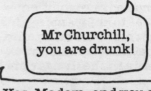

Mr Churchill, you are drunk!

Yes, Madam, and you are ugly. But I will be sober in the morning!

Steve McQueen, the Hollywood actor who performed many of his own stunts, died of cancer today in 1980.

On this day in 1951, three Himalayan climbers discovered and photographed giant footprints in the snow. The footprints were said to be made by the Yeti (alias the Abominable Snowman) and were found on the lower slopes of Mt Everest.

On 8 November 1987 a bomb blast at Enniskillen in Northern Ireland during a Remembrance Day parade killed 11 people. The bomb, hidden in an old, disused school, was planted by the IRA.

One of Britain's oldest and most famous libraries, the Bodleian, was opened in Oxford today in 1602.

Died on this day...
John Milton, the poet who wrote *Paradise Lost*. John died in 1674, and grave robbers later stole his body. **Madame Roland**, the French Revolutionary, was guillotined in Paris today in 1793.

The brewing king Alfred Heineken was kidnapped on this day in 1983. He was rescued 21 days later when police raided the parts other rescuers could not raid.

Today was a good day for British soldiers. Flogging was abolished as a punishment in the British army on this day in 1859.

Following his defeat in World

War I, the German Kaiser abdicated on this day in 1918. Wilhelm II (known in England as 'Kaiser Bill') fled to Holland and lived in the Castle of Doorn until his death in 1941.

King Edward VII was born today in 1841. His mum was Queen Victoria. Edward had to wait 60 years before he could take up the job he was born for - the time when most people retire.

And it's goodbye to...
Neville Chamberlain, the Prime Minister who tried to negotiate with Hitler. Died in 1940.
Charles de Gaulle, President of France. Died in 1970.
Dylan Thomas, the Welsh poet. An alcoholic, Dylan died in New York, 1953, after drinking one whisky too many. His final words...

> I've had eighteen straight whiskies, I think that's the record... After 39 years, this is all I've done.

NOV 10

On this day in 1928, 27-year-old Hirohito became Emperor of Japan. After the horrors of World War 2, Hirohito rejected the popular belief that the Japanese Emperor was a god.

The Moody Blues' single *Nights in White Satin* was released on this day in 1967.

Today in 1871, the journalist Henry Stanley finally met the African missionary and explorer David Livingstone in Tanzania. As they met, Stanley coined one of the 19th-century's most famous quotes...

> Dr Livingstone, I presume.

Born today...
Martin Luther, who began the Protestant Reformation and translated the Bible into German for the first time. Born in 1483.
William Hogarth, the engraver who satirized 18th-century life in England. Born

in 1679.
George II, the last English King to leade his soldiers into battle. Born in 1683.

Today is Armistice Day (also known as Remembrance Day), when Germany surrendered and World War 1 came to an end in 1918. The surrender was signed in a railway carriage at 5am in the forest of Compiegne. Hitler later used the same carriage, in the same forest, to accept the defeat of France in World War 2.

In Roman times, this was the festival of Vinalia (in honour of Bacchus, the god of wine).

Today in 1906, the first balloon crossing of the Alps took place. The balloon *Milano,* piloted by Murillo and Cresti, lifted off at Milan and passed over the summit of Mont Blanc, the highest mountain in the Alps.

Today in 1920, two years after the end of World War 1, the body of an unknown soldier was buried in Westminster Abbey. He was buried with full state honours, as a representative of all the soldiers who fell in the war.

The epic film *Ben Hur* was premiered in London today in 1959.

Ned Kelly, the outlaw and bank-robber, was hanged in Melbourne, Australia, on this day in 1880. He was 26 years old.

NOV 12

On this day in 1660, John Bunyan was arrested for illegally preaching in a barn. He spent the next 12 years almost continually in prison, where he wrote his classic, *The Pilgrim's Progress*.

Today in 1923, Adolf Hitler, an army corporal from World War 1, was involved in an attempted revolution to seize power in Munich. As the demonstrators marched through the city, a man with his arm linked to Hitler was shot dead. Hitler fled but was later imprisoned.

Chloroform was used as an anaesthetic during a British operation for the first time today in 1847.

King Canute, the Danish King who ruled in England, died on this day in 1035. Canute is remembered for getting his feet wet in the sea to show his flattering courtiers that he couldn't command the tide not to come in

NOV 13

The British aircraft carrier, *Ark Royal,* was sunk by an Italian U-boat during World War 2 today in 1941. The ship, which went down off Gibraltar, had been launched only four years earlier.

On this day in 1940, the Walt Disney film *Fantasia* received its world premiere.

Today's birthdays...
Augustine of Hippo, the

234

great Christian thinker, and the first person known who could read without moving his lips. Born today in AD354.

King Edward III, who came to the throne at the age of 15. Born this day in 1312.

Robert Louis Stevenson, the author of *Treasure Island,* was born in 1850.

> Fifteen men on the dead man's chest
> Yo-ho-ho and a bottle of rum!
> Drink and the devil had done for the rest -
> Yo-ho-ho and a bottle of rum!

NOV 14

On this day in 1952, the first British singles charts were published by the *New Musical Express.*

James Bruce, the Scottish explorer, became the first European to reach the source of the Blue Nile in Ethiopia on this day in 1770. The Blue Nile is a tributary of the main river.

Nell Gwynne, who at different times had been a comedy actress, an orange-seller, and King Charles II's favourite mistress, died on this day in 1687.

Queen Elizabeth II gave birth to a baby boy on this day in 1948. He was to be called

Charles Phillip Arthur George and was the heir to the throne.

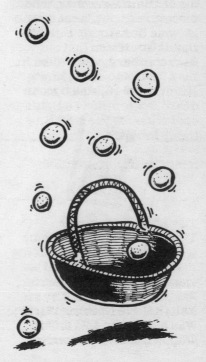

NOV 15

Today saw the first-ever BBC news broadcast, in 1922. The radio broadcast was made from London's Strand at 6pm and the newreader was Arthur Burrows.

On this day in 1875, the level of the River Thames rose by about 28 feet and caused severe flooding in London.

Today's birthdays...
Sir William Herschel, who discovered the planet Uranus in , was born today in 1738.
Count Claus von Stauffenberg, who failed in his attempt to assassinate Hitler in 1944, was born in 1907

NOV 16

The Roman **Emperor Tiberius** was born in Rome today in 42BC. It was during his reign that Jesus Christ was crucified.

The first Westminster Bridge was opened on this day in 1750. The bridge stood on the site of the present Westminster Bridge, and it replaced the old ferry that had been used to get people across the river.

Died on this day...
King Henry III at Westminster in 1272.
Clark Gable, the Hollywood film actor and star in *Gone With the Wind*. He died in 1960.

NOV 17

Today in 1558, Queen Elizabeth I began her reign. After the difficult reign of her sister, Queen Mary, the nation rejoiced at their new (and attractive) young Queen. Bells rang out all over England, and on each anniversary of this date, even after Elizabeth's death, bellringers were kept busy.

Some canal news...

The **Suez Canal** connecting the Med. with the Red Sea, opened on this day in 1869. The canal turned the continent of Africa into an island.

Meanwhile, over in the newly-dug **Panama Canal** the first ship made its way through the canal's locks on this day in 1913.

Queen Mary died today in 1558. Mary was fiercely Catholic, and had 277 Protestants burned at the stake during her reign.

NOV 18

18 November 1987: on Wednesday evening, a small fire broke out on an escalator at King's Cross tube station in London. Just after the fire brigade arrived, a fireball suddenly swept up the escalator shaft, and into the ticket hall. Thirty people were killed in the fierce heat. The fire broke out on a pre-war wooden escalator.

The bell 'Big Ben' was struck for the very first time on this day in 1858. The bell was named after Sir Benjamin Hall, and weighed 13,700kg/13.5 tons.

The funeral of the Duke of Wellington, the hero of the Battle of Waterloo, took place in St Paul's Cathedral, today in 1852. The hearse used in the funeral can still be seen in the cathedral's crypt. Wellington once said about his own army...

> I don't know aht effect these men will have upon the enemy, but, by God, they terrify me!

On this day in 1870, Pigeon Post was established between London and Paris. Paris was under siege by German troops at the time, and the pigeons helped to get news in and out. The day and night service cost 5d a word.

Mickey Mouse's first film, *Steamboat Willie*, was first shown to an audience at the Colony Theater on Broadway, New York, today in 1928.

St Peter's Basilica in Rome was dedicated today in 1626. St Peter's is 'home' to the world's one billion Catholics. It is believed to be built over the tomb of St Peter, who was martyred in Rome in AD64.

Born today...
George Gallup, the first opinion pollster. Born in Iowa, USA, in 1901.
WS Gilbert, of the humorous Gilbert and Sullivan Operas. While Arthur Sullivan wrote the music, William Gilbert wrote the words. Gilbert was born today in 1836.
Ignacy Jan Paderewski, who was both a concert pianist *and* the first Prime Minister of Poland. He was born in Poland on this day in 1860.

NOV 19

The most mysterious prisoner ever, **'the man with the iron mask'** died in the Bastille, Paris, on this day in 1703. He had spent 24 years in prison, and his identity was a closely-guarded secret. He was obviously a nobleman and the warders had orders to treat him with the utmost respect, but to kill him instantly if he removed his mask.

Born this day...
Indira Gandhi, the Prime Minister of India. Born in 1917.
King Charles I, the only English King to be tried and executed. Charles was born this day in 1600.

Franz Peter Schubert, the composer, died in Vienna today in 1828.

On this day in 1863, President Abraham Lincoln gave his famous Gettysburg Address, on the Civil War battlefield. Some of his words were...

...government of the people, by the people, and for the people, shall not perish from the earth.

NOV 20

Liz and Phil got married on this day in 1947. The church was Westminster Abbey, and they signed the register as Princess Elizabeth and Prince Philip, the Duke of Edinburgh. Their wedding cake weighed in at a modest 500lb.

The Nuremberg Trials started on this day in 1945. Twenty-four senior Nazis were tried for war crimes and crimes against humanity. The leading Nazis in the dock were Goering, Hess and Ribbentrop. Four judges and four prosecutors, representing Britain, France, the US and the USSR, ploughed through mountains of evidence at the trials.

NOV 21

On this day in 1911, women rioted in Whitehall when they were yet again refused the vote in Parliament. The windows of many government buildings were smashed as hundreds of suffragettes went on the rampage. Women were only given the vote after the end of World War 1.

This night in 1974, IRA bombs were detonated in two Birmingham pubs, killing 20 people and injuring 187 others. The bombings were the worst-ever mainland attacks by the IRA.

Born this day...
Voltaire, the French writer, born in Paris, 1694.
René Magritte, the Belgian surrealist painter with a sense of humour. Born in 1898.

Died this day...
Henry Purcell, the English composer. Died in London, 1695.

NOV 22

22 November 1963: As **President John Kennedy** was driven through Dallas in an open-top car, he was shot in the head by an assassin firing from an abandoned building. Cradled in his wife's arms, the President was rushed straight to Parkland Hospital, but 25 minutes later he was pronounced dead.

On the same day, 1963, the Beatles' first LP, *With the Beatles,* was released in Britain.

Today in 1975, the monarchy was restored in Spain. King Juan Carlos succeeded General Franco as Spain's ruler. The country had not had a king since 1931, when Spain was declared a republic.

Today's famous births...
George Eliot, the English woman novelist (her real

name was Mary Ann Evans), who concealed her identity as women weren't supposed to write novels. Born in 1819.

Charles de Gaulle, the President of France. Born in 1890.

Benjamin Britten, the English composer. Born 1913.

Boris Becker, the Wimbledon tennis champion, was born today in 1967.

Died today...
Sir Martin Frobisher, the English explorer. Died in

Plymouth, 1594.

The pirate **Blackbeard** (his mum called him Edward Teach). He died in 1718.

Sir Arthur Sullivan, the composer half of Gilbert and Sullivan. Died in 1900.

CS Lewis, the author of *The Lion, the Witch and the Wardrobe, The Screwtape Letters* and many other books. He died at home in Oxford, 1963.

NOV 23

Today saw the first episode of a new television series. Starring William Hartnell as the Doctor, *Dr Who* was broadcast from this day in 1963.

The first-ever pillar box was put up on this day in 1852. It was in St Helier, Jersey.

On this day in 1910, **Dr Hawley Harvey Crippen** was executed for the murder of his wife. He had murdered her for another woman, and they had fled in disguise to

Canada. They were arrested at sea after the captain of their ship had seen through their disguise.

Born today...
Valdemar Poulsen, the Danish inventor of the tape recorder. Val was born in 1869.

Billy the Kid, the Wild West outlaw who murdered 21 people before being shot by Sheriff Pat Garrett. His real name was William Bonney. Born in 1859.

Harpo Marx, the silent, harp-playing Marx Brother. Harpo (real name, Adolph) was born today in New York, 1888.

NOV 24

This date is remembered for occasions when the River Thames in London froze over. This happened today in 1434 and again in 1715. A frost fair was held on the ice from this day in 1715 until the following 9th of February. Drink stalls were set up, oxen roasted, etc.

Lee Harvey Oswald was shot dead in Dallas police HQ in front of live TV cameras. Oswald had just been charged with the assassination of President Kennedy, and was being transferred to prison. Oswald was shot by Jack Ruby, a nightclub owner.

Today in 1548, Parliament voted to allow clergymen in Britain to marry. Before this time, celibacy had been legally enforced.

The controversial book *The Origin of Species* by Charles Darwin was published on this day in 1859. The book presented Darwin's theory of evolution, and scandalized Victorian readers.

Born today...
Scott Joplin, the ragtime composer who wrote *The Entertainer* (the music used in the film *The Sting*) Born in Chicago, 1868.
Ian Botham, the controversial English cricketer. Born 1955.
Billy Connolly, the Scottish comedian. Born in 1942.

NOV 25

Today in 1984, a host of rock stars gathered at Ladbroke Grove, London, to record *Do They Know It's Christmas?* The song was recorded to raise money to combat the Ethiopia famine. The single went on to become the highest-selling single of all time in the UK, raising over £90 million.

Three ships became the first European vessels to sail into the waters of the Pacific Ocean this morning in 1520. The three ships were commanded by the

Portuguese explorer Ferdinand Magellan. Every man in the ships knelt as Ferdinand prayed that the waters of the new ocean would always be as peaceful as they were that morning. Then he said...

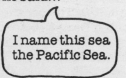

I name this sea the Pacific Sea.

On this day in 1952, a new play by Agatha Christie, *The Mousetrap*, opened at the Ambassadors Theatre in London. It went on to become the longest-running play in history. An estimated seven million people had seen the play by this day in 1987.

Born today...
Joe Di Maggio, the great American baseball player who married Marilyn Monroe. Born in 1914.
Carl Benz, builder of the first petrol-driven car, and half of Mercedes-Benz. Born in 1844.

NOV 26

Today in 1703, England experienced a Great Storm, killing an estimated 8,000 people. There wasn't another storm like it until the 'hurricane' of 1987.

On this day in 1922, the tomb of the Egyptian King Tutankhamen was opened after being sealed 3,250 years earlier in 1337 BC. Sixteen steps had been discovered leading down into the sand near Luxor, with a door at the bottom. The archaeologist Howard Carter made a hole in the door and looked inside with a candle. He was asked what he could see. He replied...

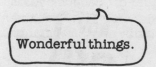

Wonderful things.

The tomb, stocked with treasures, was the most complete ever discovered.

The poet **William Cowper** was born on this day, 1731, in Berkhamsted, Herts.

NOV 27

On this day in 1703, the first lighthouse to be built on the lethal Eddystone Rocks in the English Channel was destroyed in England's Great Storm. The present Eddystone Lighthouse is the fourth to be built on the rocks.

Pope Paul VI was almost knifed at Manila airport in the Philippines, today in 1970.

Born on this day...
Anders Celsius, the man who gave us the centigrade scale. Born in Sweden, 1701.
Alexander Dubcek, political leader of Czechoslovakia until he was arrested during the Soviet invasion of the country in 1968. Born in 1921.
Jimi Hendrix, the legendary US rock guitarist. Born in 1942.

NOV 28

Today is a 'Dismal Day'. In medieval England, this day was believed to be unlucky. There are 24 Dismal Days in the year, two appearing in every month. They were also known as 'Egyptian Days'.

On this day in 1905, Sinn Féin, the political wing of the IRA, was founded in Dublin. *Sinn Féin* is Irish for 'we ourselves'.

Today in 1290, **Queen Eleanor of Castile** (the wife of King Edward I) died in Lincoln. The grief-stricken Edward set up 12 stone memorial crosses between Lincoln and London along the route of her funeral

procession, ending at Charing Cross. The crosses were placed at every point where the coffin was put down. Three still remain, at Northampton, Geddington and Waltham. The cross outside Charing Cross station is a replica.

William Blake, the poet and artist, was born in Soho, London, on this day in 1757. One of his most famous poems begins...

> Tiger! Tiger! burning bright
> In the forests of the night,
> What immortal hand or eye
> Could frame thy fearful
> symmetry?

NOV 29

On this day in 1937, the number 999 had a new meaning in Britain. From 8am today, dialling this phone number got you straight through to Scotland Yard.

Today's birthdays...
Derek Jameson, Fleet Street editor and television broadcaster, was born on this day in 1929.
Louisa May Alcott, the author of *Little Women*. Born in Pennsylvania, 1832.
CS Lewis, who wrote the Narnia chronicles and *The Screwtape Letters*. Born in Belfast, 1898.

Died on this day...
Prince Rupert, the dashing cavalier commander of Charles I's troops against Cromwell. Died in London, 1682.
Maria Theresa, Empress of Austria. Maria died in Vienna, 1780.

Cardinal Wolsey, the man who refused to get Henry VIII his first divorce, died this morning in 1530 while under arrest for high treason. He had been the most powerful man in England (apart from Henry) for 15 years. His last words...

> If I had served God as diligently as I have done the king, He would not have given me over in my grey hairs.

NOV 30

Today is St Andrew's Day (he is the patron saint of Scotland). Some Scots celebrate the day by wearing a St Andrew's Cross.

On this day in 1580, Sir Francis Drake returned from a three-year voyage around the world in his ship, the *Golden Hind*. It was only the second such voyage ever, and the first achieved by an Englishman. On the way, Drake had plundered several Spanish ships, and the Spanish ambassador demanded that he should be punished. Instead, Queen Elizabeth I knighted him on board the *Golden Hind*.

At 8pm on this night, 1936, the Crystal Palace in London caught fire and burned to the ground. The palace, a massive exhibition hall of glass and iron, had been built in 1851. Thousands of people swarmed to London to see the spectacular flames.

Today's births...
Jonathan Swift, the author of *Gulliver's Travels*. Born in Dublin, 1667.
Mark Twain (whose real name was Samuel Clemens) was born today in 1834. Twain was the author of *Tom Sawyer* and *Huckleberry Finn*.
Sir Winston Churchill, Prime Minister of Britain during World War 2. Winston was born in 1874.

Oscar Wilde died in Paris on this day in 1900. Among his last words were...

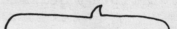

Either this wallpaper goes or I do.

NOV 31

The Beatles long-awaited reunion took place on this day in 1986. They appeared secretly at an ordinary Friday night dance at Manchester University, billed as The Comebacks. It took the stunned audience of 60 a full 10 seconds before they realized who had walked on stage.

Viking VI, the US spacecraft, soft-landed on Mars this morning and transmitted back to Earth the first signs of life on another planet. A line of large footprints was clearly visible in the soil only 20 feet from the craft.

Born on this day…
Clark Kent, shy reporter on the *Daily Planet*, Metropolis, USA. Born in 1906.
Maurice Marina, British car manufacturer, was born this day in 1976.

Dr Jekyll, the infamous Victorian murderer, died this day in 1886. Jekyll committed suicide just before he was to be arrested.

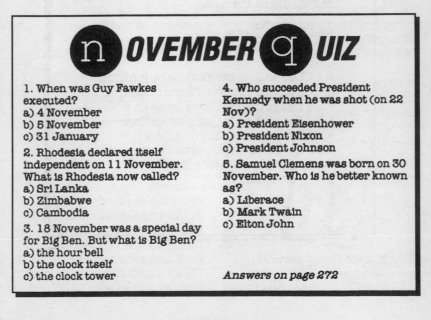

n OVEMBER q UIZ

1. When was Guy Fawkes executed?
a) 4 November
b) 5 November
c) 31 January

2. Rhodesia declared itself independent on 11 November. What is Rhodesia now called?
a) Sri Lanka
b) Zimbabwe
c) Cambodia

3. 18 November was a special day for Big Ben. But what is Big Ben?
a) the hour bell
b) the clock itself
c) the clock tower

4. Who succeeded President Kennedy when he was shot (on 22 Nov)?
a) President Eisenhower
b) President Nixon
c) President Johnson

5. Samuel Clemens was born on 30 November. Who is he better known as?
a) Liberace
b) Mark Twain
c) Elton John

Answers on page 272

DECEMBER

Name
When the ancient Romans wanted to give this month a name, they decided on December - meaning the 'tenth month'. Does this mean that the Romans were bad at maths or what?

The answer is that December used to be the tenth month, until Julius Caesar added two extra months (January and February) to the beginning of the year.

Red Letter Days
• 6 December is St Nicholas's (Santa Claus) Day
• 17 December marks the beginning of the Roman feast of Saturnalia
• 24 December is Christmas Eve
• 25 December is Christmas Day
• 26 December is Boxing Day
• 31 December is Hogmanay in Scotland, New Year's Eve for everyone else

DEC 1

David Ben Gurion, Israel's first Prime Minister, died today in 1973.

1 December marks the official birthday of the British potato. The potato was introduced into Britain by Sir Francis Drake on this date in 1586.

On this day in 1900, thousands of gallons of beer were poured into the sewers of Liverpool and Manchester. Why? Because the beer had an unusual additive - arsenic. Four people were killed as a result of drinking the poisonous brew, and a further 2,000 were injured.

DEC 2

Today in 1804, Napoleon Bonaparte was crowned Emperor Napoleon I in Paris.

On this day in 1697, the new St Paul's Cathedral was opened in London. The cathedral had been designed by Sir Christopher Wren to replace the old St Paul's, which had burned down in the Great Fire of London 30 years earlier. St Paul's is the world's largest Protestant church.

Died on this day...
Hernando Cortés, the Spanish General who conquered Mexico. Cortés overthrew the Aztec Empire and claimed the territory for Spain. He died in 1547.
The **Marquis de Sade**, the French writer who gave his name to the word sadism. Died in France, 1814.

DEC 3

On this day in 1967, the world's first successful heart transplant operation was carried out by Dr Christian Barnard in Cape Town, South Africa. The operation gave a new lease of life to a 53-year-old grocer.

William Gladstone became Britain's Prime Minister on this day in 1868.

And it's goodbye to...
Robert Louis Stevenson, the author of *Treasure Island*, and *The Strange Case of Dr Jekyll and Mr Hyde*. Stevenson died in Samoa, 1894.
St Francis Xavier, the Jesuit missionary who travelled to Japan and China. Francis died in China, 1552.
Mary Baker Eddy, who founded the Christian Science sect. She died in America in 1910.

DEC 4

On this day in 1791, *The Observer*, Britain's oldest Sunday newspaper, was first printed.

Smog (a lethal mixture of smoke and fog) descended on London today in 1962. The smog lasted for four days and killed over 60 people.

On 4 December 1981, Deuel Wilhelm Davies, a triple murderer, was given a 10,000-year prison sentence in Alabama, USA. This rather meaningless sentence is a world record. So far, Deuel has not been released for good behaviour, but he hopes to have his sentence halved.

Jean-Bedel Bokassa was crowned Emperor of the Central African Republic on this day in 1977. The Third World country he ruled footed the bill for his lavish coronation - all $30 million of it.

On the subject of enthronements, Nicholas Breakespeare was enthroned as Pope Adrian IV, today in 1154. Nicholas was the only English person ever to be made pope.

DEC 5

On this day in 1933, the Prohibition Era came to an end in the United States. For 14 years it had been illegal to sell alcohol, which had led to 'bootlegging' - the illegal supply of liquor by gangsters such as Al Capone.

King Louis XVI of France went on trial for his life on this day in 1792. In January he was sentenced to death for treason, and guillotined.

Today in 1958, Britain's first stretch of motorway was opened by Prime Minister Harold Macmillan. The motorway was the Preston bypass.

Born on this day...

General George Custer, the American general who was killed while fighting the Sioux Indians at the Battle of Little Big Horn. Custer was born in Ohio, 1839.

Walter Elias Disney, was born today in 1901. He is remembered for Mickey Mouse, Donald Duck, Dumbo, the Seven Dwarfs and Disneyland.

Died on this day...
Wolfgang Amadeus Mozart, the classical composer. He died in Vienna, 1791.
Alexandre Dumas, the French author of *The Three Musketeers,* 1870.

DEC 6

Today is St Nicholas' (Santa Claus') Day. St Nicholas lived in the 4th century AD and very little is known about him beyond the fact that he punched a heretic in the ear at an important church council. The tradition is that he threw some gold coins into the house of a poor family at night. The coins landed in a stocking that had been hung up to dry, which explains how he found his way into the Christmas tradition.

The big Christmas celebrations in countries like Switzerland and Holland happen on this day rather than on 25th December.

On this day in 1492, Christopher Columbus discovered Hispaniola, now called Haiti.

Today in 1922, Southern Ireland was declared by King George V to be a free state. The nine northern counties of Ulster remained part of the United Kingdom.

In medieval times on this day every year schoolboys elected one of their friends to be the 'Boy Bishop'. He would 'rule' from 6th to 28th December, conduct mock services and process around the town. If a Boy Bishop died during his term of office, he was buried with the full honours of a real bishop. This custom was abolished in 1542.

Anthony Trollope, the English novelist who wrote the Barchester chronicles, died in London on this day in 1882.

DEC 7

At daybreak on Sunday 7 December 1941, 360 Japanese planes attacked the American fleet at Pearl Harbour in Hawaii. The surprise attack came just days after Japan had assured America of their friendly intentions. The American fleet was crippled, and America was instantly drawn into World War 2.

Today is a 'Dismal Day'. In medieval times, this day was believed to be unlucky.

On this day in 1911, men's pigtails were abolished in China.

Captain William Bligh, the commander of HMS *Bounty*, died today in 1817. Bligh, a severe disciplinarian, was put in an open boat in the Pacific during the mutiny on the Bounty in 1789.

DEC 8

On this night in 1980, **John Lennon** was shot dead outside the Dakota building, where he lived, in New York. He was shot by 25-year-old Mark Chapman, who had asked him for an autograph that same afternoon. As Lennon and Yoko Ono entered the building, Chapman stepped out from the shadows and fired five shots at point-blank range.

Today in 1864, the Clifton Suspension Bridge was opened in Bristol. Sadly, the man who had designed it (Isambard Kingdom Brunel) wasn't there to see it. He had died five years earlier.

On this day in 1941, the United States declared war on Japan and entered World War 2. The declaration followed the Japanese bombing of the American fleet in Pearl Harbour the previous day.

Mary Queen of Scots was born in Scotland today in 1542. She was Elizabeth I's great rival to the English throne, and was executed by order of Elizabeth in 1587.

DEC 9

Today in 1960 was a milestone in television history. The first episode of *Coronation Street* was broadcast by Granada TV.

Newgate Prison in London staged its first execution at daybreak today in 1783. The execution took place before a crowd of onlookers in front of the prison gates. Public executions continued to be held there until 1868. The Old Bailey now stands on the site of Newgate.

Today's birthday persons...
Clarence Birdseye, the American frozen food pioneer. Clarence was born in 1886.
Joan Armatrading, rock musician, was born today in 1950.
John Milton, the poet and author of *Paradise Lost*. Born in London, 1608.

DEC 10

There was no 10 December 1582 in France. On this day, the French changed their calendar from the old and inaccurate Julian system (devised by Julius Caesar) to the new Gregorian system (now used worldwide). This meant they had to lose 10-19 December, jumping straight from 9 December to the 20th. Comprenez-vous?

On this day in 1901, the first Nobel Prizes were awarded. There are six Nobel Prizes: for achievements in chemistry, physics, medicine, literature, peace and economics. Famous winners include Mother Teresa, Martin Luther King and Lech Walesa (all awarded the Peace Prize). The prizes are awarded on this day each year.

Alfred Nobel (the Swedish inventor of dynamite who made millions and used the money to found the Nobel Prizes) died on this day in 1896.

On this day in 1936, King Edward VIII abdicated the throne of Great Britain after less than a year as king. He wanted to marry the American divorcee Mrs Wallis Simpson, but the Prime Minister and the Church of England objected. Edward and Mrs Simpson left for France the same day. In his abdication letter to the House of Commons, Edward said...

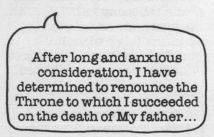

After long and anxious consideration, I have determined to renounce the Throne to which I succeeded on the death of My father...

On exactly the same date in 1688, King James II abdicated the British throne and fled by boat to France, in fear of his life. The Dutch ruler, William of Orange (shortly to become King William III) had landed at Torquay and threatened to take James's kingdom.

Llewelyn ap Gruffydd, the last Welsh-born Prince of Wales, was killed after the Battle of Aber Edw by the English on this day in 1282. From this time on, all Princes of Wales have been the eldest sons of the ruling English king.

Born today: **Alexander Solzhenitsyn**, the Russian author who wrote *Cancer Ward* and *The Gulag Archipelago*. Born in Russia, 1918.

DEC 12

On this day in 1889, George Eastman, the American founder of Kodak, produced the first celluloid roll of film. Up until this time photographers had used bulky glass plates to take pictures, but Eastman introduced portable cameras and rolls of film.

Born today...
Frank Sinatra, known as Ol' Blue Eyes, famous for his performances of *My Way* and *New York, New York*. Frank, who also starred in several films, was born in New Jersey in 1915.
Edward G Robinson, the Hollywood actor who often played gangsters in his movies. He was born in Rumania in 1893.

Died today...
Robert Browning, the English poet, died in 1889.
Douglas Fairbanks, the great swashbuckling Hollywood actor. Fairbanks swashed his last buckle on this day in 1939.

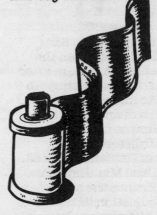

DEC 13

On this day in 1904, at 3pm, the first electrically-powered tube train left Baker Street station in London. Up until this day, underground trains had been pulled by steam engines.

Dr Samuel Johnson, the 18th-century wit and writer, died on this day in 1784. Once he had had to listen to an incredibly bad violinist murdering a piece of music. Johnson remarked to him...

Difficult do you call it, Sir? I wish it were impossible!

Dick Van Dyke, star of the American TV *Dick Van Dyke Show* and of the film *Mary Poppins,* was born today in 1925.

DEC 14

On this day in 1911, Roald Amundsen, the Norwegian explorer, became the first person to reach the South Pole. The sun was shining for the last few days of the expedition's journey.

Michel de Nostredame was born in France on this day in 1503. He is known to us as Nostradamus, the astrologer whose book, *Centuries,* is said to contain accurate predictions about the future. It is claimed that Nostradamus predicted the Fire of London, Napoleon, the French Revolution and the rise of 'Hister' (could this be Hitler?), 'a child of Germany'. Both sides in World War 2 claimed that Nostradamus predicted success for them!

Also born today: **Tycho Brahe,** the Danish astronomer who wore an iron nose after his real one was lopped off during a duel. He was born in 1564.

Died on this day...
George Washington, the first American President, who appears on all dollar bills. Washington died in 1799.
Prince Albert, the much-loved German husband of Queen Victoria, in 1861. Victoria spent the remainder of her life (40 years) in mourning for him. For years the room in which he died was kept exactly as it had been on this day. The Royal Albert Hall is named after him.
Stanley Baldwin, Prime Minister of Britain in the years leading up to World War 2. He died in 1947.

DEC 15

On this day in 1906, London Underground's Piccadilly Line was opened between Finsbury Park and Hammersmith by Lloyd George. Trains ran under the West End through the newly-designed 'tube' tunnels, cut deep underground.

Born today...
Nero, the Roman Emperor, born in AD37. Nero was a mad, cruel emperor, chiefly remembered for two things. He played the lyre (a sort of harp) while watching Rome burning, admiring the beauty of the flames while people perished. And he illuminated an evening party he gave by having Christians crucified and set alight.

Alexandre-Gustave Eiffel was born in France this day in 1832. His claim to fame was that he built the Eiffel Tower in Paris, in 1889.

Died today...
Sitting Bull, chief of the Sioux tribes. Died in South Dakota, 1890. Sitting Bull led the Sioux attack on General Custer's troops in 1876.
Walt Disney, the film animator and creator of Disneyland, died in Burbank, California in 1966. Disney's body was frozen in the hope that he could be preserved until a cure was found for the cancer that killed him.

DEC 16

On 16 December 1944, Glen Miller, the American jazz bandleader, disappeared. His plane went missing during a flight over the English Channel. His body was never found.

Today is the anniversary of the 'Boston Tea Party'. On this day in 1773, 840 chests of tea were thrown into Boston harbour in America, when Britain unfairly taxed the colonies' tea. The tea party was one of the events that led the colonies into open rebellion against British rule.

Napoleon divorced Josephine on this day in 1809.

The world premiere of the film *Chitty Chitty Bang Bang* took place on this day in 1968.

On this day in 1653, Oliver Cromwell became the Lord Protector of England in the absence of a king. Four years earlier, King Charles I had been executed for treason.

Born today...
Catherine of Aragon, Henry VIII's first wife and his first divorce case. Catherine was born in Spain, 1485.
George Whitefield, the cross-eyed, fiery Methodist preacher, was born in Gloucester today in 1714.
Jane Austen, author of *Pride and Prejudice,* was born in Hampshire, 1775.

Noel Coward, the playwright, actor and songwriter, was born in Middlesex, 1899.
Arthur C Clarke, the science fiction author who wrote *2001: A Space Odyssey.* Born in Somerset, 1917.

Died today...
Wilhelm Grimm, joint-author (with his brother Jacob) of *Grimm's Fairy Tales.* He died in Berlin, 1859.
W Somerset Maugham, the English author who wrote *The Moon and Sixpence.* Maugham was also a spy during World War 1. He died in 1965.

DEC
17

At 10.30am on this day in 1903, Orville Wright climbed into a small biplane called the *Flyer* and took off on a 12-second flight on the beach at Kitty Hawk, North Carolina. This was the first-

ever flight of a heavier-than-air plane, and marks the beginning of the age of flight.

In Roman times, today was the first day of the festival of *Saturnalia.* Slaves were allowed to do and say what they wanted, and there was a lot of feasting, drinking, practical joking and party-going. Saturnalia lasted until 23 December, and cheered up the dark days of winter.

Francis Drake sailed from Plymouth on this day in 1577 in his ship The *Pelican* - later renamed The *Golden Hind*. His voyage took him all the way around the world in just under three years. This was the first circum-navigation achieved by an Englishman.

Born today...
Ludwig van Beethoven, the tempestuous composer, was baptized in Bonn-on-Rhine today in 1770. He had been born a few days earlier. Beethoven is famous for his nine symphonies and for his piano pieces.
Sir Humphrey Davy, the inventor of a safe lamp for miners to use underground. Humphrey was born in Cornwall, 1778.

DEC 18

On this day in 1969, the death penalty for murder was abolished in Britain.

The total abolition of slavery in the United States was officially announced by Abraham Lincoln on this day in 1862.

Ex-President Gerald Ford appeared in the soap opera *Dynasty* today in 1983.

Cassius Clay, the world heavyweight boxing champion, was born in Kentucky today in 1942. He later changed his name to Muhammad Ali. He once said...

Boxing's a rough sport. After every fight I rush to the mirror to make sure I'm presentable. A lot of boxers' features change - mainly when I fight 'em!

And now some bad news and some good news...
Antonio Stradivari, the maker of stradivarius violins, died in Italy on this day in 1737. His secret of perfect violin-making died

with him. There are about 450 of his violins scattered around the world, worth about £500,000 each.
Charles Wesley was born today in 1707. Charles was one of the most prolific hymn-writers ever, and his older brother was John Wesley, the founder of Methodism. He wrote over 6,500 hymns. One of his most famous hymns starts...

> Love divine, all loves excelling,
> Joy of heaven, to earth come down...

DEC 19

On this day in 1905, the first emergency ambulance service was set up in London. Until this day, ambulances had been used only to isolate infectious patients. The new service was introduced to rush car accident victims to hospital.

The first London to Moscow air service began today in 1957.

Henry II became King of England on 19 December 1154. Henry was the king who quarrelled with Thomas à Becket, the Archbishop of Canterbury. Becket was murdered in the cathedral by four of Henry's knights.

Born today...
Leonid Brezhnev, leader of the Soviet Union from 1964 to 1982. Under Brezhnev, the Soviet Union had an icy face. Leonid was born in the Ukraine in 1906.
Eamonn Andrews, the Irish television personality who surprised countless guests on *This Is Your Life*. Born in 1922.

Died today...
JMW Turner, the British landscape artist, died in Chelsea, London, in 1851.
Emily Brontë, the author of *Wuthering Heights*. Emily died in 1848. She was 30 years old. Emily's final words...

> If you will send for a doctor I will see him now...

DEC 20

On this day in 1902, the foundation stone of the new Criminal Courts of Justice at the Old Bailey was laid by London's Lord Mayor. Judges have been handing down sentences on this site since 1773.

Born today...
Robert Van de Graaff, the American physicist. He invented the Van de Graaff Generator, capable of generating 1 million volts. Born in Alabama, 1901.
Robert Menzies, the Australian Prime Minister in the 1950s and 60s, was born today in 1894.

Died today...
John Steinbeck, the American novelist famous for his book *The Grapes of Wrath*. Steinbeck died in New York, 1968.

DEC 21

Today is Doubting Thomas's Day. Thomas is the patron saint of old people, and on this day in medieval England old people were given presents of money to help them prepare for Christmas. A children's rhyme came from this custom...

Christmas is coming and the geese are getting fat, Please spare a penny for the old man's hat!

Today is the Winter Solstice - the shortest day of the year. Although it may not feel it, from tomorrow, summer is on the way.

21 December 1988: A terrorist bomb hidden in a tape recorder exploded in a Pan-Am jumbo jet. The plane disintegrated and fell on the Scottish town of Lockerbie. There were no survivors from the plane.

On this day in 1913, the *New York World* became the first newspaper ever to publish a crossword puzzle.

Today in 1620, the Pilgrim Fathers, sailing in the *Mayflower,* landed at Plymouth Rock, Massachusetts. They were one of the first groups of British emigrants to travel to the New World.

Famous birthdays...
Jane Fonda, the American film actress and fitness fiend. Born in 1937.
Benjamin Disraeli, the British Prime Minister who charmed Queen Victoria. 'Dizzy' (as he was known) was born in 1804.
Frank Zappa, the rock musician, was born today in 1940.

DEC
22

Beethoven's 5th and 6th Symphonies were given their first performance in Vienna on this day in 1808.

Today is a 'Dismal Day' - believed in medieval times to be an unlucky day. The year conatins 24 Dismal Days.

Alfred Dreyfus, a French soldier falsely accused of passing military secrets to Germany, was sentenced to imprisonment on Devil's Island today in 1895. The prison on Devil's Island (off the north coast of Latin America) was notorious for its inhuman conditions. Dreyfus was pardoned and released in 1899.

And it's goodbye to...
Beatrix Potter, the author and illustrator of *Peter Rabbit, Jemima Puddleduck* and other stories. Beatrix died in 1943.
Richard Dimbleby, the unique television presenter who pioneered the modern style of commentary. He is especially remembered for his commentary on Elizabeth II's coronation. Dimbleby died in 1965.

DEC 23

The first circumnavigation of the globe by plane without refuelling or stopping finished at Edwards Air Force Base, California, on this day in 1986. Dick Rutan and Jeana Yeager took just over nine days to set this record in their aircraft *Voyager*.

Today in 1834, Joseph Hansom patented his horse-drawn cab in London. Joseph was also an architect (he designed Birmingham Town Hall), but he is best remembered for the Hansom Cab.

On this day in 1972, Managua, the capital city of Nicaragua, was destroyed by an earthquake lasting two hours. Two-thirds of the buildings were destroyed, and 12,000 people died.

Born today...
Joseph Smith, the founder of the Mormons (the Church of Jesus Christ of Latter-Day Saints). Joseph was born in America in 1805.
Jean François Champollion, the French archaeologist. He deciphered the famous Rosetta Stone, which made reading Egyptian hieroglyphics possible for the first time. Born in 1790.

Died today...
Thomas Malthus, the first person to predict the population explosion and to call for population control. Thomas decreased the world population by one when he died in 1834.

DEC 24

On Christmas Eve, 1818, the carol *Stille Nacht* (which is German for *Silent Night*) was written by J Möhr in Hallein, Austria. He wrote it for the village's church service the next day.

Traditionally, it was on Christmas Eve that a massive log (called the Yule Log) was hauled into the house and placed on the hearth. There it would be set alight, to burn right through Christmas Day.

On this day in 1968, three

men were further away from home than anyone had ever been before. The *Apollo VIII* astronauts were in orbit around the Moon. As millions of television viewers watched live pictures of the Moon, astronaut Frank Borman read the creation account from Genesis Chapter 1. This was probably the most unusual Bible reading of all time.

In medieval times, church bells were tolled between 11pm and midnight on Christmas Eve. This was 'The Old Lad's Passing Bell', rung to mark the death of the Devil ('the old lad') and the birth of Christ.

Humphrey Bogart, the Hollywood film actor who starred in *Casablanca* and *The Maltese Falcon,* was born on this day in 1899.

DEC
25

25 December is **Jesus Christ's** official birthday. No one knows exactly when he was born, but this is the traditional date. It all happened around the year AD4.

On this day in 1914, peace broke out in the middle of World War 1. German and British troops, who had been firing at each other only the day before, climbed out of their trenches to wish each other a happy Christmas. There was a football match, and an exchange of cigars and jam. The next day, it was war as usual...

Meanwhile, in the Pacific Ocean, Captain Cook landed on a small island this day in 1777. He named it Christmas Island.

Two kings thought that Christmas Day would be a good time to be crowned... **Charlemagne** ('Charles the Great') was crowned Emperor of the Holy Roman Empire today in AD800 by Pope Leo III.
William I ('the Conqueror') was crowned King of England in Westminster

Abbey on this day in 1066. He had won the Battle of Hastings just 10 weeks earlier.

On this day in 1906, suffragettes in Holloway Prison refused to eat their Christmas Dinner. They were protesting about the fact that women were being refused the right to vote.

White Christmases (when snow was actually falling on Christmas Day) happened in the 20th century in Britain on these dates: 1916, 1927, 1938, 1956, 1964, 1968, 1970, 1976.

Today in 1950, the stone of Scone was stolen from Westminster Abbey by Scottish nationalists. The stone, on which Scottish kings had been crowned, was taken from the Scots by King Edward I in 1296. It was incorporated into the coronation chair, and English kings have been crowned on it ever since. The stone was eventually recovered the following April.

On this day in 1957, the Queen interrupted everyone's Christmas afternoon by making her first Christmas broadcast on television.

Other birthdays that took place today...
Kenny Everett, radio and television comedian. Kenny was born on this day in 1944.
Annie Lennox, pop singer, was born today in 1954.
Little Richard, the rock'n'roller, was born in Georgia on this day in 1935.

Charlie Chaplin, silent film comedian, died on Christmas morning in 1977.

DEC 26

Today is Boxing Day, when money collected in boxes in church was distributed to the poor. This was known as 'the Box Money'.

On 26 December 1065, Westminster Abbey was consecrated. It had been rebuilt from ruins by King

Edward the Confessor, who died shortly afterwards.

Almost 900 years later, in 1955, the singer Carl Perkins recorded the ground-breaking hit, *Blue Suede Shoes*.

Today is also the Feast of St Stephen. This was the day when Wenceslas looked out...

Good King Wenceslas looked out, On the feast of Stephen...

Stephen was the first Christian to be put to death for his faith. He was stoned to death just outside Jerusalem, around the year AD30.

December the 26th is the first of the 'Daft Days'. The Daft Days were celebrated in Scotland, and took place between Christmas and Hogmanay (31 December). Excessive merrymaking took place to welcome in the new year. This day is also the first of the 12 days of Christmas. If you happen to be looking for a present to give your true love on this day, then why not visit your local pet shop and garden centre...

On the first day of Christmas, My true love gave to me A Partridge in a Pear Tree...

Mao Tse-Tung (alias Chairman Mao), leader of the Chinese Communist Revolution, was born this day in 1893.

On this day in 1717, England's first pantomime was staged at the Lincoln's Inn Theatre, London. It was given the jolly title: *Harlequin Executed*...

Oh no it wasn't!

Oh yes it was!

DEC 27

Today is St John the Evangelist's Day (he wrote the Gospel of St John). In Germany, this day used to be celebrated by drinking large quantities of German wine. Drinking the wine was supposed to make you look more attractive, and make you more healthy and famous.

The play *Peter Pan* by James Barrie first opened in London on this day in 1904.

Today in 1918 saw the first-ever visit of an American President to Britain.

President Woodrow Wilson was welcomed by King George V at Charing Cross station. The two countries had quarrelled back in the 1770s when the American states opted out of the British Empire.

On this day in 1979 the Soviet Union invaded Afghanistan, which lies on Russia's southern border. The invasion caused worldwide protest, and led the United States to boycott the Moscow Olympic Games in the summer of 1980.

DEC 28

28 December is also known as Childmas Day. It commemorates the slaughter of Bethlehem's children by King Herod at the time Jesus Christ was born.

Edward IV's coronation was originally set for this day in 1461. But it was postponed because 28 December was

considered a very unlucky day in medieval times. It was believed that any work you did or any new venture you started on this day would be bound to fail.

Chewing gum was patented in America today in 1869.

28 December 1879: As the 7.15pm mail train began crossing the newly-built Tay Bridge in Scotland, a gale smashed a 3,000ft gap in the

central section of the bridge. The train plunged into the gap and disappeared into the river, killing nearly 80 passengers. The bridge was rebuilt and the train was eventually raised from the river bed, but it was never again used to cross the bridge.

In Mexico, All Fools' Day is celebrated on 28 December rather than on 1 April. The Mexicans don't play tricks, they just borrow things, as items borrowed don't need to be returned!

And now some famous deaths...
Queen Mary II (who ruled England with King William III), died today in 1694.
Gustave Eiffel, who designed and built the 1,050-foot Eiffel Tower in Paris. Gustave died today in 1923.

Labour politician **Roy Hattersley** was born on this day in 1932.

On this day in 1170, Thomas à Becket, the Archbishop of Canterbury, was murdered in Canterbury Cathedral. Becket, originally one of King Henry II's most trusted friends, had had a long quarrel with the king. In an angry outburst, Henry shouted...

Four of Henry's knights took the king seriously and rode for Canterbury. They found Becket in the cathedral and cut him down before the high altar. Becket's final words were...

If all the swords in England were brandishing over my head, your terrors did not move me.

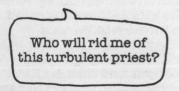

Who will rid me of this turbulent priest?

On this day in 1937 the Irish Free State became an independent country with the new name of Eire.

Dr Magnus Pyke was born on this day in 1908.

DEC 30

30 December
On this day in 1879, Gilbert and Sullivan's comic opera, *The Pirates of Penzance,* was given its first performance - at Paignton in Devon.

The last King of Romania, King Michael, abdicated on this day in 1947. He had been forced to go by the newly-elected communist government.

Gregory Rasputin, the miracle-worker at the Russian court, was murdered on this day in 1916. Rasputin, a peasant's son, had become a favourite of the Tsar's wife when he cured her son of haemophilia. Through her he had a big influence on the affairs of state. He was murdered by other members of the royal family who shot and dumped him in the river after poison had failed to have any effect.

Born today...
Rudyard Kipling, the poet and author who wrote the Jungle Book (which inspired Walt Disney's film), was born on this day in 1865. **Tracy Ullman,** comedian and (occasionally) pop singer, was born today in 1959.

DEC 31

31 December is celebrated as Hogmanay in Scotland and New Year's Eve in the rest of Britain. The Hogmanay (according to one theory) was an oatmeal cake given to the kids as they sang carols in the streets. Serious Hogmanayers still clean out the house, straighten the pictures and change all the bed sheets in preparation for the arrival of the new year. On the stroke of midnight,

the front door is flung open to allow the old year out and the new year in.

Thomas Maynard didn't have much to celebrate about on Hogmanay in 1829. On this day he became the last person in England to be hanged for forgery.

John Wyclif, who first translated bits of the Bible into English, died on this day in 1384.

Today in 1923, the chimes of Big Ben were first broadcast to the nation on the radio.

On this day in 1881, the notorious Newgate Jail in London said goodbye to its last prisoner. From this date it ceased to be used as a prison.

Last day birthdays include the following...

Donna Summer, disco queen, was born on this day in 1948.

Ben Kingsley, the film actor who played the starring role in the epic film *Gandhi*, was born today in 1943.

Bonnie Prince Charlie, who went on to lead an unsuccessful Scottish attempt to seize the English throne, was born in Rome today in 1720.

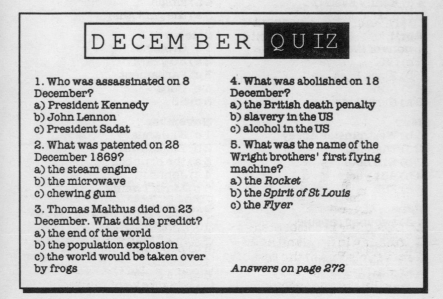

DECEMBER QUIZ

1. Who was assassinated on 8 December?
a) President Kennedy
b) John Lennon
c) President Sadat

2. What was patented on 28 December 1869?
a) the steam engine
b) the microwave
c) chewing gum

3. Thomas Malthus died on 23 December. What did he predict?
a) the end of the world
b) the population explosion
c) the world would be taken over by frogs

4. What was abolished on 18 December?
a) the British death penalty
b) slavery in the US
c) alcohol in the US

5. What was the name of the Wright brothers' first flying machine?
a) the *Rocket*
b) the *Spirit of St Louis*
c) the *Flyer*

Answers on page 272

QUIZ ❗ ANSWERS

January
1 a) eat haggis
2 a) three wise men
3 b) Omnibus
4 b) 'the cup'
5 c) Old Christmas Day

February
1 b) cheap jewellery
2 c) red-haired wig
3 c) Alphonse
4 a) Bank of England
5 b) 'dumbhead'

March
1 b) Jewish Temple
2 b) 3
3 a) blind
4 c) Kenny Everett
5 c) Saxe-Coburg

April
1 none of them
2 c) OK
3 b) Black Bess
4 c) Anne
5 a) the pillory

May
1 b) Westminster Abbey
2 c) Thailand
3 b) £10 note
4 b) 451 years
5 c) FBI

June
1 a) two-man capsule
2 c) the shower
3 a) Central Line
4 b) 'The hell I will!'
5 b) Joan of Arc

July
1 c) Salvation Army
2 c) Buzz Aldrin
3 a) Richard Starkey
4 c) *Punch*
5 b) K2

August
1 b) airmail
2 b) the Caribbean
3 c) Elvis Presley
4 a) Berlin Wall
5 b) New Amsterdam

September
1 b) Cleopatra
2 b) Neville Chamberlain
3 a) 300mph
4 a) single
5 a) the guillotine

October
1 b) Groucho
2 a) 30 years
3 c) Parliament
4 a) Cuba
5 c) 53

November
1 c) 31 January
2 b) Zimbabwe
3 a) the hour bell
4 c) Johnson
5 b) Mark Twain

December
1 b) John Lennon
2 c) chewing gum
3 b) population explosion
4 a) and b)
5 c) the *Flyer*